The Theology of the Christian Year:
The Sermons of Father Robert Crouse

THE SOUL'S PILGRIMAGE

The Theology of the Christian Year:
The Sermons of Father Robert Crouse

THE SOUL'S PILGRIMAGE

Volume I: From Advent to Pentecost

R. D. CROUSE

Volume editors: Susan Dodd and Gary Thorne

Series editors: Stephen Blackwood,
Neil Robertson and Gary Thorne

DARTON·LONGMAN+TODD

This collection published in 2023 by
Darton, Longman and Todd Ltd
1 Spencer Court
140 – 142 Wandsworth High Street
London SW18 4JJ

This collection © 2023 The Elliott House of Studies, Inc.

The right of R. D. Crouse to be identified as the Author of this work has been asserted in accordance with the Copyright, Designs and Patents Act 1988.

ISBN: 978-1-915412-42-3

A catalogue record for this book is available from the British Library.

Produced and designed by Judy Linard

Printed and bound by Replika Press Pvt Ltd, India

In Memoriam
Robert Darwin Crouse
Et erit ibi semita et via, et via sancta vocabitur.
Isaiah 35:8

Apse mosaic of San Clemente, Rome (1120-1128), 'Tree of Life'.

CONTENTS

Acknowledgements   13
Preface: Rowan Williams   17
The Timeline of the Christian Year Image   20
Note: The Timeline of the Christian Year: Gary Thorne   23
Introduction: Volume I: Gary Thorne   27

CHRIST THE KING   37
ADVENT I FIRST SERMON   41
ADVENT I SECOND SERMON   45
ADVENT II   49
ADVENT III   54
ADVENT IV   57
CHRISTMAS   62
OCTAVE DAY OF CHRISTMAS   65
EPIPHANY   70
BAPTISM OF OUR LORD FIRST SERMON   75
BAPTISM OF OUR LORD SECOND SERMON   79
EPIPHANY I   83
EPIPHANY II   87
EPIPHANY III   91
CANDLEMAS FIRST SERMON   95
CANDLEMAS SECOND SERMON   99
EPIPHANY V   103
SEPTUAGESIMA FIRST SERMON   106
SEPTUAGESIMA SECOND SERMON   111

THE SOUL'S PILGRIMAGE

SEPTUAGESIMA THIRD SERMON	115
SEXAGESIMA	119
QUINQUAGESIMA	123
ASH WEDNESDAY	126
LENT I	129
LENT II	134
LENT III	138
LENT IV	142
PASSION SUNDAY FIRST SERMON	147
PASSION SUNDAY SECOND SERMON	151
PALM SUNDAY	154
TUESDAY IN HOLY WEEK	158
MAUNDY THURSDAY FIRST SERMON	163
MAUNDY THURSDAY SECOND SERMON	167
GOOD FRIDAY	170
EASTER DAY	176
EASTER MONDAY	180
EASTER I	185
EASTER II	189
EASTER III	193
EASTER IV FIRST SERMON	198
EASTER IV SECOND SERMON	201
EASTER V/ROGATION	205
ASCENSION	209
SUNDAY AFTER ASCENSION	214
PENTECOST/WHITSUNDAY	219
TRINITY SUNDAY AND BAPTISM	224
TRINITY SUNDAY	228
Notes	233
List of Illustrations	251

Be not conformed to this world: but be ye transformed by the renewing of your mind.
Romans 12:2

ACKNOWLEDGEMENTS

The editors thank the Elliott House of Studies and the other General Editors of *The Works of Robert Crouse*, Stephen Blackwood and Neil Robertson, for trusting us with this labour of love. Henry Roper gave generously of his time and talent in preparing the final text for publication.

The editors have had the singular joy of harvesting the fruit of many labourers in the vineyard. All who were fortunate enough to hear Father Crouse preach knew that they were hearing extraordinary sermons, and many enthusiastically collected them to be re-read and shared with others. For several decades at least two Nova Scotia websites have been dedicated to making some of these sermons accessible to local preachers and pilgrims alike. The editors are grateful to these websites and to all who generously searched their private collections to contribute to these volumes.

The generosity of so many in gathering, typing, copying, scanning, and generally caring for these sermons has made it possible to produce a fairly complete set of sermons according to the ancient one-year lectionary of the Christian Year in which Father Crouse discerned a systematic theology shaped by the primitive church. Recent monographs by liturgical scholars confirm the decades-old teaching of Father Crouse that the lectionary of the Christian Year that survived virtually unchanged for over a millennium and a half until the mid-twentieth century had been fully shaped by the late-sixth/

… early-seventh century. Thus, the spiritual logic of conversion and sanctification as understood and lived by the entire Western early church can be discerned by a faithful preaching of this lectionary. Those whom we thank in the list below have helped to make known, through these sermons, the gifts of grace in the supernatural virtues of faith, hope and charity. Their work has contributed to the legacy of the teaching of Father Crouse that only when the intellect is enabled by faith to fix its vision upon the eternal Good, only when the will is strengthened by hope to pursue that Good, and only when the powers of the soul are united in an eternal Charity (that same divine *amor* which moves the sun and the other stars), will we come to know both God and our own souls. And thus we thank sincerely the following for making possible the publication of these sermons: Fr Mark Andrews, Donald Bean, Sarah Benson, Amy Bird, Fr Patrick Bright, James Bryson, Peter Bryson, Kristi Bryson, Bishop Anthony Burton, Peter Bullerwell, Erin Bullerwell, Fr David Butorac, Patricia Chalmers, Fr Barry Craig, Veronica Curran, Fr David Curry, Fr Jordan Draper, Fr Gavin Dunbar, Roger Edmonds, Marion Fry, Andrew Griffin, Hannah Griffin, Sarah Griffin, Nick Halley, Paul Halley, Fr Walter Hannam, Gwyneth Harris *requiescat in pace*, Fr David Harris, Fr Peter Harris, Susan Harris, Fr Nick Hatt, Bishop Michael Hawkins, Fr Ross Hebb, Kate Helsen, Aidan Ingalls, Fr Ranall Ingalls, Stuart Kinney, Fr Benjamin Lee, Tracy Lenfesty, Jolanta Lorenc, Thomas McCallum, Fr Colin Nicolle, Peter O'Brien, Fr David Phillips, Jeffrey Reed, Patricia Robertson, Morgan Rogers, Fr Christopher Snook, Fr Sean Taylor, Karis Tees, Fr Benjamin von Bredow, Fr George Westhaver, Virginia Wilmhoff, Lokwing Wong, and many others of the co-inherence.

ACKNOWLEDGEMENTS

The editors are responsible for the selection of sermons for these volumes. Other than that, we have merely reaped what so many others have sown (John 4:38).

PREFACE BY ROWAN WILLIAMS

To become a Christian believer is not simply to acquire a certain extra number of true statements in one's mind; it is to enter a new environment, to see new sights and learn new songs, to understand in a wholly new way who one is and who the neighbour is. My own story of how I have grown to be the person I now am is taken up into an incalculably larger story, the narrative of *how God brought God's own life to be*, within the compass of the created world. What happens to me as a believer, the way I now – by grace and faithfulness – grow further into God's purpose, is shaped by this context: who I am is Christ (and who the neighbour is is Christ). It is a shocking and daring affirmation, and we should not be surprised if it takes time to sink in and is not instantly intelligible to our usual mayfly-like attention span. But year by year, the Christian community patiently leads us through the story, familiarising us once again with the extraordinary truth that our lives are now wrapped up in the identity of Christ.

The story of the Christian year lays out that identity, step by step. Christ is the one who is longed for as the fulfilment of promise, the one who fulfils the divine promise by embracing the entirety of human nature, who lives out his divine Sonship in and through the pains and struggles of the human condition, who embraces death so that his fellow-human beings may live, and whose life and act proves deeper and more real than death

THE SOUL'S PILGRIMAGE

itself; who breathes on his friends the gift of sharing his divine Sonship and reveals that the mystery of reciprocal gift and love is the very shape of the eternal Godhead. It is in the midst of this that we find who we are and who we are invited to be, who our human neighbours are and are invited to be, what human society might be if transfigured by the Spirit that animates Christ's body on earth. And alongside that monumental and cosmic story, the community remembers those in whose lives this great pattern has come alive in tangible and arresting form, the company of witnesses who share and enrich our own confused, stumbling efforts to journey more deeply into this new world.

The joy of reading Fr Crouse's sermons is that they leave us in no doubt that this exhilarating landscape is a home in which we are constantly being nourished into Christlike life. We discover the truth of who we most deeply are by learning to live with the steady rehearsal, year by year, of both the great shared story and the specific records of holiness that give it added vividness and attraction. Fr Crouse was a priest and theologian exceptionally at home with the riches of that tradition shared by orthodox Christians across the Christian world, the classical deposit represented by writers from Irenaeus to Dante, Maximus to Aquinas, and beyond. We are a bit less confident these days than we once were about appealing in traditional Anglican fashion to the belief of the 'undivided Church'; and there is reason for this, as it is no great help for us to entertain pleasing fictions about some lost Golden Age of Christian thought and practice. But the pendulum must not be allowed to swing too far: there *is* a deposit of continuous and coherent wisdom, informed by prayer and liturgy as well as intellectual endeavour, which still sustains a common language between Christians divided by historical quarrels or rivalries.

PREFACE BY ROWAN WILLIAMS

At its best, the Catholic Anglican enterprise has sought to take its stand on this. Fr Crouse's preaching and scholarship – like that of Austin Farrer, rightly one of his heroes – showed that this enterprise could still work vigorously and convertingly for modern minds. This collection, leading us through the 'year of grace' that is the Christian calendar, will rekindle some confidence in this shared, prayerful wisdom; and like all good preaching it will set us free to praise the God whose life is, miraculously, gloriously, ours in the gift of Christ's Spirit.

+Rowan Williams

PILGRIMAGE: THE CHRISTIAN YEAR

Exploding Star

Christ-child teaching

The Scream

Christmas · Pre-Lent

**Advent
(December)** · Epiphany · Lent

Nativity icon

Sower of the Word

Cosmic Shepherd

Easter　　　Ascension　　St John the Baptist　　Trinity/Pentecost　　　　　　　　　　November

　　　　　　　　　Whitsunday

'Noli me tangere.' 　　　　　Preaching to the birds 　　　Vision of Paradise

NOTE:
THE TIMELINE OF
THE CHRISTIAN YEAR

To help contextualize these sermons for those unfamiliar with the historic Christian Year we have provided an illustrated timeline to help you grasp the Christian Year at a glance. We have chosen a few images to indicate that the Christian Year is simultaneously cosmic and personal in scope. These images range from ancient to contemporary: from a 2023 photograph from the James Webb Space Telescope of an exploding star 15,000 light years away corresponding to Advent, an Eastern icon of the Nativity, a twentieth-century stained glass window of Epiphany in the chapel where many of these sermons were preached, the Pre-Lent theme shown in Van Gogh's *Sower,* Lent's Edvard Munch iconic depiction of our contemporary demons in *The Scream,* a Renaissance painting of Jesus' post-resurrection caution 'Noli me tangere' ('Do not touch me'), an early fifth-century mosaic of the risen Christ as the cosmic shepherd, and Giotto's thirteenth-century painting of St Francis and the birds representing the communion of saints. The timeline concludes with a diagram of heaven's celestial rose as described in Dante's fourteenth-century poem, the *Paradiso.* The appropriateness of these images for their place on the timeline will become clear in your reading of the sermons.

The early thirteenth-century walking labyrinth of Chartres Cathedral appears above the horizontal timeline to correct the

THE SOUL'S PILGRIMAGE

impression that the Christian Year is simply linear in character. Rather, the Christian Year is a cyclical and continuous path of pilgrimage for the Christian soul, drawing the pilgrim ever nearer to the centre of discipleship with Jesus. Better still is to imagine the Christian Year as a spiral, combining both the linear and the cyclical. The 'soul on pilgrimage' ever repeats the Christian Year in this life as the end of one year becomes the fresh beginning of the next, each time at a higher (or deeper) level. This famous medieval labyrinth of Chartres represents the integrity of the created order, and its center is surrounded by a six lobed rosette that appears in Sumerian, Babylonian, Jewish, and Roman art, reminding us that our journey into the life of God is comprehensive of a universal divine seeking that is common to all peoples at all times. Jesus Christ is the cosmic Alpha and Omega, the beginning and the end, the first and the last (Revelation 22:13).

But what is so remarkable and beautiful for Christians of the twenty-first century who are seeking to put on the mind of Christ (Philippians 2:5) is that the Christian Year carries with it the *consensus fidelium* of the Church both doctrinally and liturgically. The *consensus fidelium* is the agreed 'common mind' of the faithful in relation to the revealed Word of God. In the first two centuries of the common era the canon of the New Testament was established by the *consensus fidelium*. The *consensus fidelium* then formulated the Nicene Creed (the Apostles and Athanasian Creeds soon to follow) as well as the universally accepted Ecumenical Councils culminating in the definition of the Person of Christ in the Fourth Ecumenical Council in 451 CE. Finally, by the end of the sixth century the *consensus fidelium* in the West had established the Christian Year, including a lectionary of fixed Epistle and Gospel lessons for all the Sundays and Holy Days of the year. This remarkable lectionary, shaped by the thinking

THE TIMELINE OF THE CHRISTIAN YEAR

and worship of the early Church, articulated a clear systematic theology that was embraced by the entire Western Church until the sixteenth century, and which continued unimpaired throughout the Reformation period in the Roman Catholic, Lutheran, and Anglican Churches. Thus the Christian Year with its accompanying one-year lectionary remained virtually unchanged from the sixth to the mid-twentieth century.

The Creeds and Councils of the early Church established the boundaries of Christian believing that was faithful to the Scriptures. To complement these doctrinal standards, the Christian Year with its lectionary of Bible readings was developed by the early Church as a practical pilgrimage that would guide the Christian soul into a continuing conversion and deepening life of holiness. This same spiritual pilgrimage undertaken with Jesus to the Father is available to us today. We can still join with the countless Christians from the sixth to the twentieth century, the illiterate and impoverished to the scholarly and elite, who have journeyed the path that you will discover in these sermons. Volume I is a collection of sermons that preach the first half of the Christian Year, Advent to Pentecost, rehearsing what God in Christ has done *for* us in Christ. Volume II preaches the second half of the Christian Year, focusing on what God in Christ does *in* us by the power of the Holy Spirit, shown marvellously in the lives of his saints. These saints show us the way to holiness and service.

Through the whole of the Christian Year our adoration of the saving work of God the Son *for us* leads to the renewal of our minds and hearts by the power of the Holy Spirit *in us*. Thus the pilgrimage of the Christian Year can become the journey of our soul to its home in God.

May it be that for you.

Gary Thorne

INTRODUCTION: VOLUME I

The frontispiece to this volume, the apse mosaic of San Clemente, Rome (1120-1128) is an ideal introduction to the preaching of Father Robert Crouse. For Crouse, this mosaic, in concert with the art and architecture of every age of the Church, reflects the Christian life as it is guided by the Holy Spirit. This mosaic is part of the *consensus fidelium*, the long-established common mind of the Church, in relation to the revealed Word of God. Crouse would encourage every potential visitor to Rome to visit San Clemente and have its floor pavements guide the visitor as pilgrim to the extraordinary dance of images and symbols of the apse. The significance of these are successively unveiled in his sermons throughout the Christian Year. The central cross of the apse is the Tree of Life (*lignum vitae*) and the surrounding mosaics tell the story of salvation in terms of God's divine pilgrimage. It begins in his Son's incarnation, proceeds through the created cosmos, and concludes in his redeeming sacrifice on the cross. In his preaching Crouse recalls the legend illustrated here that the cross on which Christ was crucified was made from the wood of the Tree of Life in the Paradisal Garden, thus highlighting that all of nature, and indeed the entire cosmos is redeemed through Christ's obedience. This same obedience repairs the disintegration of the cosmos caused by the original disobedience in the garden. Crouse likewise describes the

THE SOUL'S PILGRIMAGE

leaves of Christ's tree of obedience as being 'for the healing of the nations.' Alluding to historical events in the Church, the apse mosaic shows a radical diversity of persons sheltered under the huge acanthus that represents the entire Church or the vineyard of the Lord. The blood of Christ waters the vine from which is produced the blood of the Eucharist, effectual for the sanctification of the faithful. In Crouse's preaching the white doves representing the Holy Spirit may be variously seen as the twelve Apostles or as the souls of all the redeemed. The Trinity is completed in the mosaic by the descending hand of the Father. In his sermons Crouse often recalls the poetry of the sixth-century poet Venantius Fortunatus to describe the kingship of Christ precisely in the manner shown in the apse: Christ reigns and triumphs from the tree, overturning our mistaken earthly longings for the truly heavenly. The signs of his glory are body broken and blood poured out. In the apse we see the four doctors of the Church, as well as martyrs, confessors and common everyday people, all of whom find their place in the sermons of Crouse. I am suggesting that in reading these sermons you will strangely come to feel at home with these mosaics, and ultimately with the entire Christian tradition in which we live and love in the life and co-inherent love of God the Holy Trinity. Robert Crouse makes the past present such that the glory and the challenge of every age becomes our glory and the challenge to our contemporary living.

In 1930, when Robert Crouse was only a few months old, his family moved from his birthplace in Winthrop, Massachusetts back to Crousetown, Nova Scotia, a small village near the ocean. When Crouse was six his mother died of tuberculosis and he moved into his grandparents' home

INTRODUCTION: VOLUME I

next-door where he lived until his death in 2011, excepting the years when he was studying or teaching abroad. He attended a one-room schoolhouse next to the village church before going 'up the road' for junior matriculation at King's Collegiate School in Windsor, Nova Scotia, the oldest private residential school in Canada (founded in 1788). Then it was on to Dalhousie University and King's College in Halifax where he studied Classics, Philosophy, and Theology. His lifelong and unrelenting commitment to social justice became evident in his undergraduate Halifax years as he organized a 'revolutionary cell' of the Society of the Catholic Commonwealth. The Society promoted an understanding of Christianity that is redemptive of the entire natural and social order, a response to the encroaching individualist pietism of Christianity and the emerging therapeutic lens to the faith that increasingly would serve that individualism. Rather, members of the Society read Augustine, Aquinas, and Marx.

Crouse went on to Harvard Divinity School where he earned his Baccalaureate in Sacred Theology with a term abroad to study German theology at Tübingen. In 1954 he was ordained priest in his home province of Nova Scotia. He then made his way to Trinity College, Toronto, where he tutored and earned a Master of Theology in 1957 with a dissertation on 'St Augustine's Doctrine of *Justitia*' (i.e., of divine justice/righteousness). After teaching Patristics for six years at Bishop's University in Quebec, Crouse returned to Nova Scotia to teach in the Classics Department of Dalhousie University. From 1963 until his retirement as Emeritus Professor more than thirty years later, Crouse was blessed with exceptional colleagues at Dalhousie with whom he forged a manner of studying ancient and medieval texts in their original languages that attended to the logic and argument of the texts themselves, thus allowing these texts to come into a dynamic dialogue with contemporary thinking. The Classics Department reached far beyond the ancient Greek and Roman worlds to the development of ancient philosophy in the thinking of the Middle Ages. This approach opened up the logic of the philosophical texts themselves and encouraged countless students not only to study classical literature, but also to come to a rare appreciation of the Middle Ages as the indispensable connection between the ancient and modern worlds that unveils an understanding of the roots of contemporary culture.

In 1970 Robert Crouse's critical edition of the *De Neocosmo* of Honorius Augustodunensis, the most popular twelfth-century theologian and one of the most widely read of all medieval authors, earned him a PhD from Harvard. His many acclaimed scholarly journal articles published over his academic career covered a broad spectrum of interests and demonstrated his interdisciplinary approach. Each article was a finely-honed argument which might include aspects of philosophy, history, theology, literature, architecture, or poetry. In the early 1970s Crouse helped to establish a highly successful distinctive great books programme at the University of King's College that emphasized the Christian Latin Middle Ages as an essential period in the development of modern notions of human freedom and personhood. Crouse continued to give lectures in the Foundation Year Programme on medieval architecture and music, and on the *Confessions* of St Augustine, well after his formal retirement. His lectures on Dante's fourteenth-century poem, the *Divine Comedy* became perhaps the best-loved and the core of the King's Foundation Year, inspiring students to experience the love that moves

INTRODUCTION: VOLUME I

the sun and the stars as the same love that enlightened and fired their intellectual curiosity. In 1977, Crouse co-founded a respected scholarly journal, *Dionysius,* that focuses on the history of ancient philosophy and theology, including Patristic theology. In 1990 Crouse became the first non-Roman Catholic to be invited to teach at the *Institutum Patristicum Augustinianum* in Rome where he continued as visiting Professor in Patristics until 2004. King's College awarded Crouse an Honorary Doctor of Divinity in 2007, his second. In the citation for his first DD *(honoris causa)* received from Trinity College Toronto in 1983, Crouse was described as 'the conscience of the Canadian Church'.

'The conscience of the Canadian Church' was an apt description of how Robert Crouse would continue to contribute to the life of the Church. As Bishop Victoria Matthews writes in the forward of volume two of these sermons, Robert Crouse 'cast a critical vision on the global Church'. Wherever and whenever the Church falsely embraced the universal Word made flesh as her own possession in a narrow denominationalism, in an individualistic piety that was less than the conversion of the entire cosmos, in a forgetting of her Patristic, Medieval, and Reformation tradition, or in a spirit of triumphalism, Crouse's preaching gently reminded the Church of her fuller identity. In his annual scholarly theological addresses at the Atlantic Theological Conference, which he co-founded in 1983, in his occasional retreat addresses to priests and laity, and in his sermons, Crouse recalled the Church to her universal mission. His sermons are Anglican only in the older notion of an Anglicanism that refuses to be narrowly confessional, but rather true to the spirit of the ancient councils and creeds that were first forged in the healthy dialogue with (and often embrace of) the philosophy of the Greeks, and then further illuminated in conversation with her sister Abrahamic faiths and Eastern philosophies throughout the Middle Ages. Crouse preached from the one-year lectionary of fixed readings for Sundays and Holy Days that had been fully formed and shaped by the end of the Patristic period. This lectionary was almost unchanged throughout the Western Church to the time of the Reformation, and then continued in its integrity through the sixteenth-century Reformation to the mid-twentieth century in the Roman Catholic, Lutheran, and Anglican Churches.

With few exceptions these sermons were preached in a 30-year period between 1975-2005, to a wide diversity of persons, of various occupations and educational backgrounds, in one of three pulpits: a sophisticated middle-class urban church of liberal tendencies, a small traditional fishing village church, and the chapel of a secular liberal arts university. It was as a student at the University of King's College in Halifax that I first heard Father Crouse preach in the mid-1970s. As students, most of us were uninterested in formal religion. We were pre-occupied with our own issues of self-identity, friendship, and love. Regardless, we were convinced by other students (who looked for all the world to be no more 'churchy' than we were) to come to the university chapel to hear this quiet, otherworldly, erudite preacher. What we heard was local and simple, yet at the same time cosmic and profound: a broad philosophical wisdom at one with Gospel teaching, applied practically to our contemporary friendships and loves. It was clear that the preacher's remarkable intellect was filtered through a deeply pastoral spirit. We heard of the offering of a divine and human friendship that was inclusive of every form of human desire

INTRODUCTION: VOLUME I

and love as articulated throughout two millennia of Christian theology, poetry, art, sculpture, architecture, and music.

Those sermons in that university chapel led countless students to friendship with Father Robert, a true contemplative who lived simply in his Crousetown home where his family had resided for more than 200 years. There, in an old-world kitchen on a chair worn and frayed from countless other visitors, perhaps the Canadian philosopher George Grant, a local farmer, or an enthusiastic young student might sit with a cup of tea recovered from the hearth. His or her eye might glance up at the scripture verse elegantly carved around the kitchen just below the ceiling, '*Et erit ibi semita et via, et via sancta vocabitur…*' ('And a highway shall be there, and a way, and it shall be called, The way of holiness.' Isaiah 35:8) The guest would look out over an inviting garden that at Robert's death boasted 129 varieties of roses. Our gracious host delighted in serving up salads created from dozens of the herbs and plants through which you had meandered by a path to his door. An organist, harpsichordist and choir director, Robert helped to inspire the rescue of the last historic tracker organ in Nova Scotia to be installed in the local village church where he hosted a baroque summer concert series that did not miss a season for 47 years. He played the organ faithfully in his small village church for decades. Finally, whether the context be classroom, pulpit, rose-garden or organ bench, Robert's gift of friendship seemed to be an invitation for each of us to embrace and share with him the rich, deep, and contemplative spiritual life that he embodied.

And we gladly accepted.

Gary Thorne
Feast of the Annunciation, 2023

THE SOUL'S PILGRIMAGE

Notes for the sermons are presented at the back of the book. These indicate the scripture accompanying the sermon and references to other works that Fr Crouse quotes. We have presented the sermons in the main text without footnotes or citations, so that the reader may encounter them as closely as possible to how they were received when preached. The texts that we share here are simply the notes from which Father Crouse preached.

The Theology of the Christian Year:
The Sermons of Father Robert Crouse

THE SOUL'S PILGRIMAGE

CHRIST THE KING SUNDAY NEXT BEFORE ADVENT

*Jesus said unto his disciples,
Gather up the fragments that remain,
that nothing be lost.*

Today is the last Sunday of the Church's year. Next week we shall begin a new year with Advent Sunday; and we shall begin the year in solemn and joyful expectation: 'Behold, thy king cometh unto thee.' 'Hosanna to the Son of David; Blessed is he that cometh.' That's the way the Church's year begins, and that's the way the year proceeds. We are made witnesses to the kingship of Jesus: in his life and ministry, in his Passion, in his resurrection and enthronement. He calls us, and enables us, by the Spirit's gifts, to seek and find his kingship and his kingdom in our own minds and hearts and lives, here and now, here in our midst. And in that long succession of Sundays after Trinity, the Church sets before us, in prayer and scripture lessons, an ordered pattern of spiritual growth, that his kingdom – his kingdom of the Spirit – might be fulfilled in us.

'Thy kingdom come, thy will be done, on earth as it is in heaven.' Thy kingdom come, in us.

Therefore today, as we come to the year's conclusion, it is fitting that we should make a pause, and make a kind of summing up, before we set out upon that road afresh; that we should gather in, as individuals and as a community of believers, the harvest of God's grace, and offer it at the feet of Christ our King.

The Gospel lesson anciently appointed for this Sunday, before the feast of Christ the King was introduced, actually made the same point. It was St John's account of Jesus feeding the multitudes in the wilderness: the sign of his feeding us with spiritual nutriment in the wilderness of this world. But remember how that story ends: 'When they were filled, he said unto his disciples, "Gather up the fragments that remain, that nothing be lost." Therefore, they gathered them together, and filled twelve baskets with the fragments of the five barley loaves.' The twelve baskets, of course, stand for the twelve tribes of the new Israel, God's kingdom of the Spirit. Every fragment of spiritual good, all the gifts of God's superabundant grace, are to be gathered in, and treasured in his kingdom: that nothing be lost.

But the kingship of Christ is not easily understood. A strange ambiguity attends the concept through every step of the Gospel record, from Bethlehem to Calvary: from King Herod's frantic slaughter of the Innocents to Pilate's nervous question, 'Art thou a king then?' and Jesus' cryptic answer, 'Thou sayest it.' The crowd in Pilate's hall had screamed their hypocritical protest, 'We have no king but Caesar'; but then, finally, upon the cross, the title was inscribed, in Greek, and in Latin, and in Hebrew, for all the world to see, 'Jesus of Nazareth, King of the Jews.'

What a strange kingship! Who could understand it? Certainly not Herod, and certainly not Pilate; but, you know, even the disciples, even the friends and intimates of Jesus, couldn't understand it. Do you remember that story of James and John, the sons of Zebedee, and the request their mother made of Jesus, that her two sons might sit, one on his right hand, and the other on his left, in the coming triumph of his kingdom? And remember

CHRIST THE KING

Jesus' answer: 'The princes of the gentiles lord it over them, and they that are great exercise authority upon them, but it shall not be so among you.' It shall not be so among you. 'But whosoever will be great among you, let him be your minister; and whosoever will be chief among you, let him be your servant.' His kingship is a kingship of humility and obedience, a conception which turns the worldly standpoint of the disciples upside-down.

And think of the accusation against St Paul and his Christian converts in Thessalonica: 'These that have turned the world upside down are come hither also ... saying that there is another king, one Jesus.' The Jews and the Roman authorities could see the kingship of Jesus only in terms of worldly power. And all through history, too, many Christians have made exactly that mistake, seeing in Jesus' kingship only the possibility of a better sort of worldliness.

Surely that is not the Gospel, and that is not Jesus' kingship. 'Now is my kingdom not from hence,' he says. 'Now is my kingdom not from hence.' He does, indeed, turn the world upside-down, but not in the way that Herod or Pilate or the Thessalonian authorities supposed. The ways of his kingdom are much more radical than they could imagine: He turns our whole world, our whole perspective, our whole way of seeing the world and living our lives upside-down and inside-out.

'Blessed, happy, are the strong and prosperous,' says the law of worldliness. 'Blessed are the poor in spirit, those who know their own wretchedness,' says Jesus. 'Blessed are the powerful and forceful,' says the world, 'for they get what they go after.' But 'Blessed are the meek and gentle,' says the law of Jesus' kingdom, 'they shall inherit the earth.' 'Blessed are those who are full of the world's goods,' says the worldly law. 'Blessed are they that hunger and thirst for righteousness,' says Jesus, 'for they shall be filled.'

THE SOUL'S PILGRIMAGE

'Blessed are the clever,' says the world. 'Blessed are the pure in heart,' says Jesus, 'for they shall see God.' 'Blessed are ye when men shall revile and persecute you ... for great is your reward in heaven.'

'Whosoever will be great among you,' says Jesus, 'let him be your minister, and whosoever will be chief among you, let him be your servant.' The kingship of Jesus is the kingship of a servant, the kingship of humble obedience, and that is the kingship to which he calls all who would follow him. 'Inasmuch as ye have done it unto one of the least of these my brethren ye have done it unto me.'

The signs of Jesus' glory are the signs of his humility, the signs of body broken and blood outpoured: 'He reigns and triumphs from the Tree.' That is the strange kingship we venerate, and that is the glory we show forth day by day in the Church's liturgy, as we break the bread and drink the cup. And that is the glory that must adorn our lives if we would truly acknowledge Christ as king. 'Let this mind be in you, which was also in Christ Jesus.' That is the renewal of mind to which the Gospel calls us, that we should follow the example of his great humility and thus become true and faithful citizens of his kingdom. Our Christian year is our witnessing his kingship, and our emulating that kingship in our lives, by his grace. And thus we pray today that he will stir up our wills to set out afresh upon that road, plenteously bringing forth the fruit of good works, and plenteously rewarded, knowing that every fragment of spiritual good is gathered in and treasured up in his kingdom: His kingdom, to whom with the Father and the Holy Spirit, one God, be all honour, all glory, and all majesty, now and throughout all ages.

Amen.

ADVENT I
FIRST SERMON

My house shall be called the house of prayer.

With this first week of Advent, the new Church year begins in a spirit of solemn expectation, and the Epistle and Gospel lessons for this week both sound an urgent and demanding note. 'The night is far spent, the day is at hand,' says St Paul. 'Let us therefore cast off the works of darkness, and let us put on the armour of light. Let us walk honestly as in the day.'

The realm of nature, at this season, declines into the darkness and the frozen sleep of winter. But, in the midst of this world's darkness, we are called to rouse ourselves, to awake from sleep, to live the new life of the spirit, to walk in the light and warmth of grace, to be ready and watchful for our salvation. And therefore, says St Paul, we must 'cast off the works of darkness'; we must clear up the clutter of our lives. Only one thing is important he says – that we let God's love rule our hearts and inform our lives. Nothing else really matters, he tells us: 'Owe no one anything, but to love one another: for he that loveth his neighbour hath fulfilled the law.'

'Let us walk honestly, as in the day, not in rioting and drunkenness, nor in clambering and wantonness' – those placebos of the senses, those ersatz satisfactions which never satisfy, 'nor in strife and envying. But put ye on the Lord Jesus Christ, and make not provision for the flesh, to fulfil the lusts thereof.' 'Nothing but love,' says St Paul. Not sentimental feelings, mind you, that's not what he means by love. Not sentimental feelings, but the earnest steadfast willing of the good that is the armour of light, and, by God's grace, we had better wake up and put it on.

We must let the love of God rule our hearts: that is the message of St Paul, in the Epistle and that is also the message of this week's Gospel lesson. Perhaps that Gospel lesson seems a strange passage to read just now, because, after all, it's really about Palm Sunday, isn't it? It's all about Christ's entry to Jerusalem at the time of his Passion. It seems to belong to Holy Week, and not at all to Advent Sunday. And yet, the Church, since ancient times, has introduced the Advent season with this text, and I think that if we consider carefully the meaning of the text we can see how precisely right it is for Advent Sunday.

Jerusalem is not just one city among others. The scriptures endow it with a rich spiritual symbolism. 'Vision of Peace' is the meaning of its name. It is the symbol of God's kingdom, the city of God's peace, the place where God reigns. God comes to his city, meek and lowly in Christ, to be acclaimed its monarch.

'Behold, thy king cometh unto thee.'

No outward show proclaims his power and divinity; he comes, 'meek and lowly, riding upon an ass'. He comes to make his city his possession. And 'all the city was moved, saying, Who is this?' 'This is Jesus the prophet of Nazareth of Galilee.' Only the eye of faith can see that this is God with us, Emmanuel. And that, you see, is a perfect parable of Advent.

'And Jesus went into the temple of God' and purged it from corruption. 'He cast out them that sold and bought in the temple, and overthrew the tables of the moneychangers, and the seats of them that sold doves; and said unto them, "It is written, 'My house shall be called the house of prayer'; but ye have made it a den of thieves".'

What is the meaning of the temple? The temple, at the city's heart, is the place where God is worshipped. It is the place of praise and adoration. It is the symbol of the city's spirit. But it is something more; it is the symbol of the human mind and heart, the human soul, whose joy and duty is the worship of Almighty God, 'in spirit and in truth'. What this cleansing of the temple means is that the advent of the Son of God implies the cleansing of our souls of all those false and worldly aims, all those works of darkness and dishonesty, all those fleshly occupations – all their busyness and trafficking which rob God of the worship that we owe him.

We have made, and continually do make, his temples dens of thieves.

So here, then, in this Gospel lesson, is the meaning of this season: 'Behold, this king cometh unto thee.' God comes to us in Christ, in his eternal Word. He comes to us, not with show of worldly power, but in meekness, as an infant in all the helplessness of his self-giving love. He comes in love and mercy; and therefore, Advent is a season of rejoicing, and we greet him with hosannas.

But his coming must also be a judgement on a city that will not know him … 'He comes unto his own', on the temple – a judgement on the darkness of our hearts, our futile dreams, our miserable pretensions, the useless clutter of our lives. He finds his temples dens of thieves. And therefore, Advent is a solemn time of preparation – that by his own grace, by his own cleansing Word, the temples of our souls may be made fit places of his worship, fit to discern, and to embrace, and to adore the mystery of love which is his coming.

THE SOUL'S PILGRIMAGE

We all know, I'm sure, something of the beauty and the joy of Christmas. There is miracle and mystery about it, which all the attendant worldly cacophony can never quite obliterate. But for most of us, I think, perhaps precisely because we have some sense of the spiritual dimension of the festival, there's also, year by year, a haunting sense of disappointment, a sense of spiritual opportunity lost somehow amidst the pseudo-mirth and busy occupations of the season.

And thus our Advent liturgies and scriptures call us urgently to prepare ourselves with prayer and penitence, to prepare our minds and hearts to adore the mystery and miracle of Bethlehem. 'Knowing the time, that it is now high time to awake out of sleep,' time to cast off the works of darkness, and arm ourselves with light, that the eternal Word of God may come to birth in the dark stables of our minds and hearts, that our poor souls may, by his grace, be dwelling places of his spirit, temples of his praise. 'For it is written,' he says, 'My house shall be called the house of prayer.'

Amen.

ADVENT I
SECOND SERMON

Owe no one anything, but to love one another.

Today the Church begins a new year. We turn back in our prayer books from the last of those Sundays after Trinity to the first Sunday in Advent and begin again that cycle of prayers and lessons which sets before us those mighty works of God in which our salvation is effected. For us and for our salvation the Son of God is made flesh – for us he dies and rises and upon us is Spirit bestowed.

Today we begin a new year – and we begin it with the solemn and urgent instruction of St Paul in today's Epistle:

> Owe no one anything –
> Knowing the time –
> The night is far spent
> Let us walk honestly …

I wonder that anyone can read these words, or hear them proclaimed, without being profoundly moved by them – because it seems to me that they speak so sharply and directly to our condition. Surely for most of us life seems very complicated indeed. Perhaps especially at this time or year, as the commercial world begins its kind of preparation for Christmas, we are reminded more forcibly than ever of the clamouring and insatiable appetites of the senses.

THE SOUL'S PILGRIMAGE

And the strife and envying of which St Paul speaks – all the petty jealousies, the grudges, the backbiting, the flattery, the jockeying for position and respectability, the suspicious and mean and petty criticisms, the struggle for worldly goods – all this seems sometimes to constitute the very fabric of our life. And all this is precisely what St Paul means when he speaks of the lusts of the flesh.

Give it up, he says – cast off the works of darkness – let us walk honestly as in the day. Owe no one anything but to love one another. Give it up – wake up – you are asleep. Not in that sleep which is quiet rest but in that sleep which is delusion – nightmare – in which there is no rest but only conflict and incoherence.

Wake up – the Lord is at hand. The day of God's truth, of God's judgement, breaks in upon our dreaming.

> Tell ye the daughter of Sion
> Behold thy King cometh unto thee.

Jesus comes to Jerusalem – God comes to his city – to our city – to the very heart of it – to the Temple – and he finds it a den of thieves.

> And Jesus went into the Temple…
> My house shall be called the house of prayer.

One thing is needful – that we walk honestly in the daylight of God's truth. But we, we have made his temple a den of thieves – that is to say, we have stolen away the goods of God's city – of his kingdom – and perverted them to construct the nightmare city of illusion.

ADVENT I SECOND SERMON

But the Lord is at hand – he overturns our tables of thievery. The night is far spent – wake up!

Thus we begin the Church's new year with a solemn and urgent warning – wake up and get your house in order. Only if we can purify our lives – only if we will cast off the works of darkness – only if we are ready to wake up – to unclutter our lives of those prejudices, those pettinesses of worldly ambitions, those lusts of the flesh, will we be able to see and know that true king who comes as the infant of Bethlehem with nothing – nothing but rags and love.

And only if we can die to our lusts will we be able to see and know the dying of the Son of God – and only if we die with him can we also rise with him – wake up to newness of life in the powers of his free spirit.

It is this that is set before us step by step in the cycle of the Church's liturgical year that we may see it and know it and have part in it – and it is this that is set before us week by week as we celebrate this holy sacrament. For here, too, God comes to his Bethlehem – his house of bread. Here, too, we represent ever and again his dying and rising – 'For as often as ye eat this bread, and drink this cup, ye do shew the Lord's death till He come.' Let us wake up and open our eyes to the renewal of life he brings.

Most of us here this morning have followed the Church's year many times, most of us have made many communions. Has it made much difference in us? Perhaps that is not a question we can very easily answer. Waking up can be a slow and painful process and we often slip back. The instant, obvious, salvation widely proclaimed around us is perhaps a rather superficial thing. We must be recalled again and again. Again and again we fall back into our daydreams and nightmares.

THE SOUL'S PILGRIMAGE

But we walk by faith, and we can't measure our spiritual achievement as, for instance, one might measure one's expertise in arithmetic. We walk by faith and we have our Lord's promise that those who truly seek will find; that no honest effort is ever finally lost. We have his word that our Father, when we ask him for bread, will not give us a stone. Let us, then, ask for bread – the very bread of life – for he will be asked for nothing less.

Amen.

ADVENT II

And when these things begin to come to pass,
Then look up, and lift up your heads;
for your redemption draweth nigh.

The spirit of the Advent season is one of hope and solemn expectation, as we prepare ourselves for the coming of our Lord and saviour. We are as watchmen, waiting in the shadows of the night for the dawning of a new day: Looking for the rising of the sun of righteousness to scatter all the chill and darkness of our minds and hearts. We hope for deliverance from the bondage of our sins and manifold perversities; deliverance from the blindness and deafness of our earth-bound souls; we hope for a new and higher life in God's kingdom of righteousness and peace. Advent speaks to us of the hopes of countless ages coming to fulfilment:

> And lo, already on the hills
> The flags of dawn appear
> Gird up your loins, ye prophet souls,
> Proclaim the day is near:
> The day in whose clear-shining light
> All wrong shall stand revealed.
> When justice shall be throned in might,
> And every hurt be healed.

THE SOUL'S PILGRIMAGE

The coming of the Son of God is our salvation, and therefore Advent is a season of rejoicing: 'Rejoice in the Lord always, and again I say, Rejoice.' But the coming of the Son of God is also our judgement, and therefore Advent is a time of watchful penitence, and we wear the purple vesture of solemn preparation. Precisely that ambiguity marks today's Gospel lesson: redemption and judgement. The lesson is part of Jesus' speech to his disciples in the Temple, in which he prophesies the destruction of Jerusalem:

> And as some spake of the Temple, how it was adorned with goodly stones and gifts, he said, 'As for these things which ye behold, the days will come, in which there shall not be left one stone upon another which shall not be thrown down. And when ye shall see Jerusalem compassed with armies, then know that the desolation thereof is nigh. This generation shall not pass away until all be fulfilled.'

That dire prophesy was, indeed, fulfilled, when the armies of the emperor Titus destroyed the city, in 70 AD, and it has been fulfilled many times in subsequent centuries. But the prophecy is not only about the destruction of Jerusalem; it is about the passing away of all created things, it is about the end of history, about the coming of Christ 'in power and great glory,' and the triumph of his kingdom.

> 'There shall be signs in the sun and in the moon and in the stars: and upon the earth distress of nations, with perplexity, the sea and the waves roaring; men's hearts failing them for fear, and for looking after those things which are coming on the earth: for the powers of heaven shall be shaken.

ADVENT II

And then shall they see the Son of Man coming in a cloud with power and great glory. And when these things begin to come to pass, then look up, and lift up your heads, for your redemption draweth nigh... When these things come to pass, know ye that the kingdom of God is nigh at hand.'

In the destruction of Jerusalem, in the devastation of the world, in the distress of nations, and the failing of men's hearts, comes redemption. In the passing away of heaven and earth, God's kingdom comes in power. In the destruction of all worldly hope and confidence, another hope arises, and the Son of Man appears in glory.

The Advent message, the message of today's Gospel lesson, about the end of things and the coming of Christ in glory, is a difficult matter. What does it mean? There are always preachers, of course, who make their calculations of the end: for next week, or next year, or for one millennium or another; and there are always people ready to go off to some wilderness or some mountain top to await the end. The Christian imagination has so often been tempted to give precision to the prophesy. One thinks of the Montanists in ancient Phrygia, the Joachimites in medieval Europe, the Anabaptists in Reformation times, Revivalists in nineteenth and twentieth-century America, and so on, right down to our own day, when television evangelists warn us about 'this end-time'. The signs are always propitious, it seems; but still the world goes on, and when they say, 'here is Christ', or 'there is Christ', we are scarcely moved to go forth.

But the prophecy of Christ's coming is an essential aspect of the Advent message. What are we to make of it? Can we not read the signs of his coming?

THE SOUL'S PILGRIMAGE

> He spake to them a parable, 'Behold the fig tree, and all the trees, when they now shoot forth, ye see and know of your own selves that summer is now nigh at hand. So likewise ye, when ye see these things come to pass, know ye that the kingdom of God is night at hand.'

The signs are always propitious, it seems: Distress of nations, with perplexity, and fearful hearts. These are no uncommon experiences; they are our daily diet. But that, you see, is precisely the point: in each and every moment, our world is passing away; each and every moment has a finality for us, for each and every moment places us under the judgement of the Word of God. It is not our business to calculate the end of time; it is our business to live this moment as those who know that each moment stands under God's judgement: 'knowing the time, that it is now high time to awake out of sleep'; discerning the coming of the Son of God in this and every moment: his coming in his holy Word, his coming in his holy sacraments, his coming to us in one another. 'And take heed to yourselves,' says Jesus, 'lest at any time your hearts be overcharged with surfeiting and drunkenness, and cares of this life, and so that day come upon you unawares.'

In the destruction of Jerusalem, in the devastation of the world, in the distress of nations, and the failing of men's hearts, comes redemption. 'When these things begin to come to pass, then look up, and lift up your heads, for your redemption draweth nigh.'

It is not in worldly hopes and ambitions and confidence that we see God's coming. He comes as a helpless infant, judging our pretensions. It is not in schemes for worldly utopias that his kingdom comes; he is cradled in a stable. It is when we know our own insufficiency, hearts failing us for fear, that we learn to

ADVENT II

look up, and hope in the promises of God. And then, indeed, he comes, 'in power and great glory.'

As Richard Crashaw puts it (in *'Carmen Deo Nostro'*):

> O see, so many worlds of barren years
> Melted and measur'd out in seas of teares.
> O see, the weary liddes of wakeful Hope
> (Love's Eastern Windowes) all wide ope
> with curtains drawn,
> To catch the Day-break of Thy Dawn.
> O dawn at last long look't for Day!
> Take thine own wings, and come away.
> Lo, where Aloft it comes!

Amen.

ADVENT III

It is required in stewards that one be found faithful.

In the season of Advent, our attention is focused upon the coming of the Lord: his coming as our saviour and our judge. We are as servants, who await a master, sorely delaying. We watch and wait. And on this third Sunday of Advent, the Church's liturgy presents us with the figure of St John the Baptist – John the baptizer – as the great example of one who watched and waited.

We know very little, really, of John the Baptist, the preacher in the wilderness of Judaea, clothed in camel's hair, and a girdle of skin about his loins: 'the voice of one crying in the wilderness: prepare ye the way of the Lord, make his paths straight.' It is sometimes supposed that he must have belonged to one of the radical sects of Judaism, such as the community of Qumran, which produced the 'Dead Sea scrolls'. The Qumran community was a group of people who had separated themselves from the mainstream of Jewish life, and had gone to live in caves by the Dead Sea, awaiting the coming of the Messiah with intense expectation. Perhaps John came from such a group. At any rate, he was one of those who watched and waited for the fulfilment of the mystery of God's promises. He was a minister and steward of the mystery of God's coming in Christ. He watched and waited, and that mystery was revealed: 'Art thou he that should come, or look we for another?' ... 'Go and show John again those things ye do hear and see' – the prophecies are fulfilled.

As John was witness to the promise, so the Apostles were

ADVENT III

witnesses to its fulfilment in Christ: 'Even the mystery which hath been hid from ages and from generations, but now is made manifest to his saints: to whom God would make known what is the riches of the glory of this mystery among the Gentiles; which is Christ in you, the hope of glory.' The mystery of God's coming to us, the mystery of God's presence with us and in us, the hope of glory.

In the Epistle for today, St Paul argues with the Christian converts at Corinth. Some of them claim to be followers of Paul, some another preacher called Apollos. St Paul tells them that all that is nonsense: 'Who then is Paul, and who is Apollos, but ministers by whom ye believed? ... Let a man so account of us as of the ministers of Christ, and stewards of the mysteries of God.' That is to say, the mystery of Christian faith, the mystery of 'God with us', is not the invention of Paul or Apollos – it is there in Christ, once for all. The Apostles are simply its ministers and stewards, and their task is to be faithful to that revelation. They are not judges of that mystery, picking and choosing, redesigning and 'improving', deciding what 'works best', and so on; rather, they are its servants. Judgement belongs to the Lord.

St John the Baptist is our Advent example, for it is our vocation too, to be ministers and stewards of the mystery of God's coming – it is our vocation, too, to watch and wait. And in our time, as much as ever, perhaps even more than ever, it is required in stewards that one be found faithful.

Faithfulness to the mystery is no easy matter. The world is always ready with other ideas: ideas for redesigning and improving, ideas about what works best, ideas about what is more relevant to our times and customs. It is not easy for us, really, to think of ourselves as servants of a truth revealed so long ago. Even some of our theologians tell us that we have reached maturity now, and have no need of the old authority;

THE SOUL'S PILGRIMAGE

we have grown up – we can judge for ourselves now. Well, it's an engaging notion, perhaps, but surely the evidence of our religious maturity is less than overwhelming.

There are those who would persuade us that the old forms of Christian belief and life are antiquated and irrelevant: we must keep up with the times, and redesign our creeds and institutions in accord with current fashions. There are those who claim that a 'new spirit' is abroad (or maybe it's not really so new); but the advice of St John is good, when he says, 'Beloved, believe not every spirit, but try (test) the spirits, whether they be of God: because many false prophets have gone out into the world.' I don't think we are very good at testing the spirits.

It would be nice to be able to say with St Paul, 'it is a very small thing that I should be judged of you, or of anyone's judgement', but in fact, it is uncomfortable and disagreeable to be out of step with the times. 'But it is required in stewards that one be found faithful' – simply that: faithful to the mystery revealed in Christ.

We prepare ourselves to rejoice in Christmas, because it shows us that amid all the confusions and uncertainties of our lives, amid all the fancies and fads of this world's gyrations, there is the fact of God's coming – the revelation of the mystery of God with us – the mystery of which we are ministers and stewards; servants of a returning Master, 'who both will bring to light the hidden things of darkness and will make manifest the counsels of the hearts'.

As a very ancient hymn expresses it:

> Happy those servants, whether he returneth
> At dead of midnight, or at early morning;
> Happy those servants, if he only find them
> Faithfully watching.

Amen.

ADVENT IV

*Behold the Lamb of God which taketh away
the sin of the world.*

'Behold the Lamb of God.' With these words John the Baptist points beyond himself and his ministry to Jesus who has come to John for baptism. Despite baptizing Jesus, John knows his greatness: 'his shoe's latchet I am not worthy to unloose.' John is a Jew. He does not become a disciple of Jesus. He is beheaded by Herod as a consequence of his own ministry which denounced sin and preached the baptism of repentance. Jesus tells us that the least in the kingdom of heaven is greater than John, yet John is indispensable to the Advent of that kingdom. John's virtue, one which we must all imitate, is that he knew what he was not and thus what was needed, what should be demanded of God, for what the soul should long. His reply to the Jewish priests and Levites was profoundly negative: He confessed:

> 'I am not the Christ.' And they asked him,
> 'What then? Art thou Elijah?' and he said,
> 'I am not.'
> 'Art thou the prophet?' and he answered,
> 'No.'

He knew what he was not. He had no delusions, he recognized what he was lacking, and he was not afraid to let others see it. He let his softness, his yielding, his vulnerability be known to all men. Expecting, hoping, and longing for the coming of the power of God's kingdom he was willing to let his need be known so that it could be supplied, so that he could be filled with a greater power and strength than his own. Today St Paul rouses us both to rejoice in the coming of the Lord and 'by prayer and supplication with thanksgiving to let our requests be made known unto God.'

John knew what he and the world lacked, and his life was devoted to longing for and calling for that justice and righteousness which he did not possess. He recognized the dryness and barrenness of this own goodness, demanded of God that he come from on high and fill that desert with life: 'I am the voice of one crying in the wilderness, prepare ye the way of the Lord, make his path straight' and so he recognized the Lord when he came. The Lord, the Messiah, the Christ came as the fulfilment of John's desire.

Let us today on the eve of Christmas learn this from John that if we are to know the coming of the Lord, we must in fact want Him to come. We must know and acknowledge what we need and lack, and have the humility to pray for it, to long for it with our whole being. If Christ is to be born in us, there must be a place prepared for Him.

But how can we prepare a place? Why is there always in us a need and longing for God, a place only He can fill?

St John the Divine tells us that the Lamb of God to which John the Baptist points is the 'Lamb slain from the foundation of the world'. God's love for us did not begin 2000 years ago. It is the eternal purpose of God to join mankind to Himself forever. This is the great eternal fact which the coming of Jesus reveals and makes known in time. 'God has chosen us in Christ before

ADVENT IV

the foundation of the world that we should be holy and without blame before Him in love.'

The eternal purpose and everlasting love of God is that men and women should enjoy His infinite goodness forever. We long for and desire God and cannot avoid this because He loves us and wants us for Himself. We love Him because He first loved us. Because He loves us, we find that all the bread and drink of this world is untrue. It cannot in the end feed our hunger or quench our thirst. We seek true bread, true drink, the bread that comes from heaven and is born in Bethlehem because the all-powerful love of God is always drawing us to God's goodness. But this love of God is costly for Him. We know that the Lamb of God, his innocent goodness which takes away our sin and makes us acceptable in God's presence, we know that this Lamb of God must be slain. The child born in Bethlehem will be raised on a cross outside Jerusalem.

Christmas is inseparable from Good Friday. The Lamb who takes away the sin is to be slain.

As John Donne put it:

> The whole life of Christ was a continual passion;
> Others die martyrs, but Christ was born a martyr.
> His birth and his death were but one continual act,
> and his Christmas Day and his Good Friday are but
> the evening and morning of one and the same day.

'The Holly and the Ivy' makes the same point:

> The holly bears a berry,
> As red as any blood,
> And Mary bore sweet Jesus Christ
> To do poor sinners good:

THE SOUL'S PILGRIMAGE

> The holly bears a thistle,
> As sharp as any thorn,
> And Mary bore sweet Jesus Christ
> On Christmas Day in the morn:
>
> The holly bears a bark,
> As bitter as any gall,
> And Mary bore sweet Jesus Christ
> For to redeem us all.

We cannot carol Jesus on Christmas unless we recollect the blood of his Passion, and the thorns of his crown, the gall of his crucifixion. For these are the high cost of eternal love of God shown and adored in the babe of Bethlehem. At Bethlehem, God works in time to serve his eternal loving purpose to take mankind into himself and to share his goodness with us forever.

The same eternal will required the sacrifice of his Son as the cost of God's high Passion for us sinners. From eternity the Son shared God's love and undertook to pay the price.

> Lo it is written in the Book,
> I came to do thy will, O God.

The man at whom John the Baptist points is the Lamb slain from the foundation of the world. We come to God through the sacrifice of love he has made from the beginning. This sacrifice is made present to us in this season in the remembrance of the humility of Almighty God coming to us as a child. This same sacrifice is made present here this morning on the altar. Eating the bread of eternal life and drinking the cup of everlasting

ADVENT IV

salvation may we taste how good the Lord is, and tasting his goodness may we so long for him as to welcome him always and welcoming him may he make us worthy to sing the eternal praise of the God who eternally loves us, Father, Son, and Holy Spirit whose kingdom is forever and ever.

Amen.

CHRISTMAS

And the Word was made flesh, and dwelt amongst us:
and we behold his glory —
the glory as of the only begotten of the Father —
full of grace and truth.

There are many surprising things about Christmas — about God's coming to us at Bethlehem. He who is the mighty God, the all-powerful, comes as a helpless infant, wrapped in swaddling clothes, lying in a manger. He who is the great king of all the earth takes upon himself the form of a servant, comes unhonoured and unknown to an insignificant village in an obscure corner of the Roman Empire. He whose praise is sung by the music of the heavens, comes in the silent midnight, silent as the April dew falling on a flower. He who is the framer of the world, the maker of the gold and precious things which adorn the halls of the rich, has nowhere to lay his head. He who is Creator of all things, comes to a life of poverty — comes to hunger in the wilderness. He who is the final judge, comes to be judged by wicked men. He in whom all things have life, comes to die the bitter death of the cross.

In all this, no doubt the purposes of God are revealed: but how are we to understand it — how can we make sense of it? Perhaps, first of all, what it adds up to is a mighty lesson in humility — God has chosen the weak things of this world to confound the strong — by coming as a helpless infant, he shatters our pretentions of wisdom and maturity: by his helplessness he

CHRISTMAS

shames all our striving for security. He shows us the emptiness of the struggle for wealth and power, for prestige and vainglory – the ways of God he shows us to be the humble and the lowly paths which lead to denial of self. Even in his infancy, he shows us the way of the cross. Thus in the birth of Christ, God shows us the emptiness of a vanity of life as most of us live it most of the time. He shows us that the things which finally count most are humility, obedience – self-denial.

He shows us the truth about human life.

God who at various times and in various ways spoke in times past to our fathers by the prophets has now in these last days spoken to us by his Son – to show us the truth. But to show us the emptiness of all the world counts most important is scarcely good news, is it? If that were all Christmas were about, we shouldn't be here singing songs of rejoicing. We should be here in sackcloth and ashes of repentance.

The message of Bethlehem is not just a devastating criticism of our sins – it is also, and above all, a message of hope and salvation. God shows us the truth about our lives and shatters our self-righteousness; but at the same time, he shows us the way out – a new life in God – for in and through Jesus Christ we can receive the grace of God, God's power to live new lives of real meaning. He is not simply the teacher, the schoolmaster, showing us our faults – exhorting us to do better. He comes to Bethlehem to be with us every step of the way, in strength to guide us out of a world of confusion and false values – to lead us home. He who is the way is also the wayfarer.

What then is the mystery of Christ's birth? It is, in the words of St John the Divine, simply this: 'Behold the tabernacle of God is with me, and they shall be his people and he will be their God.' God's Son who for us all and for our salvation came down from heaven and was incarnate by the Holy Ghost of the Virgin Mary and was made human, offers to us his life, in the ongoing life of his body, the Church. Because of Bethlehem, we have here, in Word and sacrament, the way to God. From Jesus Christ, we have received, as St Paul says, grace and apostleship, for obedience to the faith among all nations.

And therefore we rejoice in the remembrance of Christmas: For here in this festival God has given us truth and grace. We rejoice that we have seen the glory of God in the face of Jesus Christ. We rejoice that light has shined upon us, that God has shown us the way of salvation, the way of our final peace with God. The Word, the eternal Son of God, is made flesh and dwells among us, and we behold his glory; the glory as of the only begotten of the Father, full of grace and truth.

Therefore, let the heavens rejoice and let the earth be glad before the Lord, for He is come.

Amen.

OCTAVE DAY OF CHRISTMAS

The people that walked in darkness have seen a great light: they that dwell in the land of the shadow of death, upon them hath the light shined.

The prophet Isaiah, in today's Epistle lesson, speaks of the restoration of the kingdom of Israel:

> For unto us a child is born, unto us a son is given: and the government shall be upon his shoulder. Of the increase of his government and peace there shall be no end, upon the throne of David, and upon his kingdom; to order it, and to establish it with judgement and with justice from henceforth even for ever. The zeal of the Lord of Hosts will perform this.

Isaiah's words are a great outburst of rejoicing. The yoke of oppression has been broken, and a child has been born to sit upon David's throne – a great statesman, a mighty warrior, a father to his people. The prophet speaks of the coming Messiah, in prophetic fashion, as though it had already happened, and his soul is ecstatic with his vision of the Messiah's glory.

There has been, and there still is, a good deal of debate about the precise meaning of these ancient prophecies. But

THE SOUL'S PILGRIMAGE

the New Testament is abundantly clear that they are fulfilled in Jesus Christ, and that is the way in which Christian tradition has always understood them. The promised child is the child of Bethlehem, Emmanuel, God with us. He is the promised Messiah, and he sits upon David's throne as the saviour of his people; and therefore his name is 'Jesus', which means 'saviour of his people'.

The prophecies are fulfilled in Jesus Christ. By his words and by his works he makes that claim. Remember the question of John the Baptist, when he sent his disciples to ask Jesus, 'Art thou he that should come, or do we look for another?' And Jesus' answer: 'Go and show John again those things which ye do hear and see.' By words and signs he shows himself to be the Messiah, 'he that should come'.

Jesus fulfills the prophets. But in doing so, he also transforms them, and gives them a deeper spiritual sense. He comes to restore the kingdom, no doubt; but the kingdom he restores is a kingdom of the spirit. He comes to break oppression, but the oppression which he breaks is not the oppression of Babylon or Rome, it is not the oppression of flesh and blood; it is the deeper, and altogether more hateful and devastating oppression of deceitful lusts and vain ambitions. The captivity from which he frees is the captivity of the confused and wayward human soul, the captivity of sin and hopelessness.

No doubt, all this sounds pretty obvious, and even platitudinous. And yet, it seems to me that these things must be said again, and thought about again. Multitudes of our contemporaries, even multitudes of Christians, live entirely in terms of worldly hopes. Some of them are, no doubt, noble and altruistic hopes: hopes for a better world, hopes for peace and prosperity for all, hopes for comfort and security. They are

OCTAVE DAY OF CHRISTMAS

in some sense Messianic hopes: but their limit is the kingdoms of this world, and therefore their end is destruction and hopelessness. 'Here we have no continuing city.'

This is the season of Saturnalia, the ancient pagan festival of the winter solstice – the Kalends of January, according to the Roman calendar. On that festival the pagans celebrated the return of the sun, and the growing of the light. Our holy season of Christ's nativity coincides with that pagan festival, and the coincidence of the symbolism is excellent. But what we celebrate is the rising of a better sun, and the growing of a light which shines unto life eternal.

The true Messiah comes to free us from all worldly limitation, to open to us an eternal kingdom of the Spirit, which moth and rust cannot corrupt, and which no thief, except our own folly, can ever steal.

The Venerable Bede, an eighth-century English monk, in his *Ecclesiastical History of the English Nation*, tells the story of the conversion to Christianity of Edwin, King of Northumbria. The story includes a debate in Witan, the King's palace, and one of the King's nobles makes this speech:

> Such seemeth to me, my Lord, the present life of men here in earth (for the comparison of our uncertain time to live), as if a sparrow should come to the house and very swiftly flit through; which entereth in at one window and straightway passeth out through another; while you sit at dinner with your captains and servants in winter-time; the parlour being then made warm with the fire kindled in the midst thereof, but all places abroad being troubled with raging tempests of winter rain and snow. Right for the time it be within the house, it feeleth no smart of the

THE SOUL'S PILGRIMAGE

winter storm, but after a very short space of fair weather that lasteth but for a moment, it soon passeth again from winter to winter and escapeth your sight. So the life of man here appeareth for little season, but what followeth or what hath gone before, that surely know we not wherefore if this new learning hath brought us any better surety, methink it is worthy to be followed.

The true Messiah comes, and he brings us a 'new learning' and 'better surety' of a kingdom not made with hands, eternal in the heavens. 'The people that walked in darkness have seen a great light: they that dwell in the land of the shadow of death, upon them hath the light shined.'

In today's Gospel lesson, we have St Luke's story of the shepherds, hastening to Bethlehem, 'to see this thing which is come to pass … And when they had seen it they made known abroad the saying which was told them concerning this child. And all they that heard it wondered at those things which were told them by the shepherds. But Mary kept all these things, and pondered them in her heart.'

The world was indeed astonished by the remarkable story the shepherds had to tell; but we, we who have worshipped at Christ's manger, let us, with Mary, treasure these things, and ponder them in our hearts.

Amen.

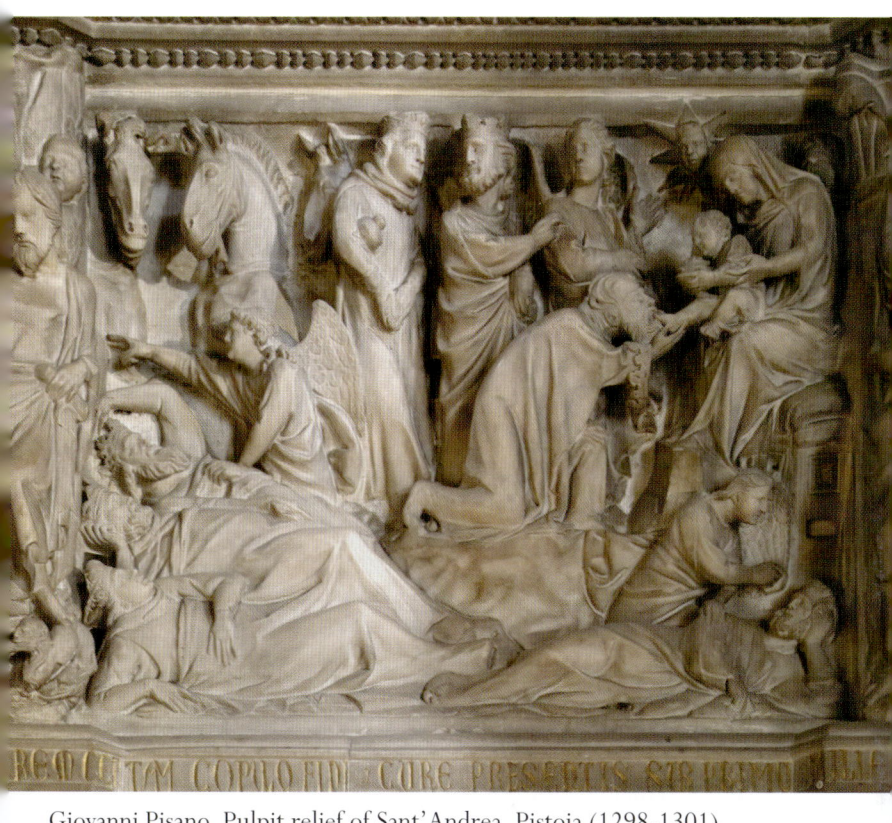

Giovanni Pisano, Pulpit relief of Sant'Andrea, Pistoia (1298-1301), 'Adoration of the Magi'.

EPIPHANY

They departed into their own country another way.

> A cold coming we had of it,
> Just the worst time of the year
> For a journey, and such a long journey:
> The ways deep and the weather sharp,
> The very dead of winter.

Thus T. S. Eliot, great twentieth-century American and English poet of 'The Waste Land,' begins his first expressly Christian poem, 'Journey of the Magi', slightly paraphrasing a few lines from Lancelot Andrewes' 'Sermon for Christmas Day, 1622'. For Eliot, the newly converted poet, now five years after writing 'The Waste Land', just lately baptized and confirmed, the ancient story of the Magi becomes a parable of conversion: a parable of his own and everyone's pilgrimage to Christ. It's a journey through a wintry desert, with refractory camels and unreliable camel-men, through hostile towns and cities, and 'with the voices singing in our ears, saying/That this was all folly.' It's the cold and hazardous journey through the waste land to a new and different world.

But what of the journey's end, the destination? According to Eliot's imagination, the travellers arrive at dawn in a temperate valley, below the snowline; a valley 'smelling of vegetation/With a running stream and a water-mill beating the darkness/And

EPIPHANY

three trees on the low sky.' There's an old white horse, galloping away in a meadow; there's a tavern, with vine leaves over the door; and one can see, within, hands dicing for pieces of silver, and feet kicking empty wineskins. It's a landscape of symbols as complex, as suggestive, and as obscure as a Bruegel painting. There are symbols of new life and transformation, mixed with symbols of betrayal, futility, and death. It's a world which, as Eliot says, seems to have 'no information' about its own meaning. It's Jerusalem below, Jerusalem in bondage with her children. Its symbols are fragments of a meaning which lies beyond it.

And so we move on, to discover – 'at evening, and not a moment too soon', says the poet – behind the ambiguity of the symbols, a fundamental paradox, in which life and death are strangely identified.

> All this was a long time ago, I remember,
> And I would do it again, but set down
> This set down
> This: were we led all that way for
> Birth or Death? There was a Birth, certainly,
> We had evidence and no doubt. I had seen birth and death,
> But had thought they were different; this Birth was
> Hard and bitter agony for us, like Death, our death.

Birth and Death: Christ's birth, our death; Christ's death, our birth. Terrible paradoxes, certainly; and they lie at the very heart of Christian faith and life. Living we die, and dying, we live. Birth and death are the two sides of every transformation, and Epiphany is about a transformation. The Son of God is manifest, and 'we all, with open face beholding as in a glass the glory of the Lord, are changed into the same image from glory to glory,

THE SOUL'S PILGRIMAGE

even as by the Spirit of the Lord'.

'Changed into the same image': transformed by adoration. No longer conformed to this world, but (as St Paul says) 'transformed by the renewing of your mind'. That renewing, that transformation in us, is a continual dying and a continual rebirth. In Christ, we die, that we may live in him: that is the mystery of our redemption; that is the mystery of this liturgy we celebrate. 'For ye are dead,' says St Paul, 'and your life is hid with Christ in God.' That's the point that Eliot picks up in the concluding lines of his poem:

> We returned to our places, these kingdoms,
> But no longer at ease here, in the old dispensation,
> With an alien people clutching their gods.
> I should be glad of another death.

Eliot's meditation on the journey of the Magi is certainly peculiar. There's no mention of the star, no mention of Herod and the scribes, no mention of the gifts, and no mention – except very obliquely – even of the mother and child. And yet, the poem grasps the essence of the story: it's the story of conversion, the story of faith's journey through the waste land, to find the Word of God behind all the ambiguities of human words, to taste the life of God in bread and wine, to find death in life, and life in death, to adore the mystery of divine love manifest, and to be transformed thereby.

Thus if 'The Waste Land' was a meditation on the futility and failure of desire, 'Journey of the Magi' is about the redemption of desire, the renewal of desire at a higher level of perception and aspiration, by the grace of Christ's Incarnation: 'we all, with open face beholding as in a glass the glory of the

EPIPHANY

Lord, are changed into the same image from glory to glory, even as by the Spirit of the Lord.' … 'No longer at ease in the old dispensation': transformed by adoration.

'The Waste Land' and 'Journey of the Magi' represent the two sides of Christmas: the two sides liturgically represented in Advent and Epiphany. Advent sets before us the divine judgement upon a God-forsaking, and therefore seemingly God-forsaken world: 'The Day of the Lord of hosts,' cries the prophet, 'The Day of the Lord of Hosts shall be upon all pleasant pictures' (or more literally, 'upon all pictures of desire'). That is the waste land. But it is to that ruined and ruinous world that redemption comes: 'When these things begin to come to pass,' says Jesus, 'then look up, and lift up your heads, for your redemption draweth nigh.' It is in the waste land that the divine thunder speaks, it is in the wilderness that the Lord's coming is prepared. All that is Advent.

Epiphany, on the other side of Christmas, looks upon the glory of that coming, now fulfilled: 'we behold his glory,' says St John, 'the glory as of the only begotten of the Father, full of grace and truth.' And all the lessons of this Epiphany season illustrate the facets of that glory, manifest in signs and wonders: signs of divine wisdom and divine power – Jesus with the doctors in the Temple; Jesus turning water into wine at the wedding feast at Cana; Jesus healing the leper and the Centurion's servant – signs of the glory of God manifest in Jesus Christ. But the vision of that glory is a transforming vision; we are transformed by adoration: 'changed into the same image … even as by the Spirit of the Lord.' … 'We returned to our places, these Kingdoms/ But no longer at ease here', says Eliot: no longer conformed to this world, but transformed by the renewing of our minds.

'Where is he that is born king of the Jews?' Where is the

THE SOUL'S PILGRIMAGE

Son of God, who comes to save us? Where is that bread of life for which our spirits faint? Faith bids us find him, as it were, in a stable. Faith bids us find the Word of God in human words; faith bids us taste the very life of God in elements of bread and wine; faith bids us meet and serve the Son of God in one another – in the least of these, his brethren; to see and to declare his glory shining there. There, you see, is Bethlehem for us, now and always. There is Epiphany for us; there his glory shines, and there we make our gifts of adoration.

And so, if we make our own winter journey to Christ; if we do behold our Lord and saviour, there in Bethlehem, and adore him there, we do not return unchanged. We do not return to Herod; transformed by adoration, we go home 'another way'.

'They departed into their own country another way.'

Amen.

BAPTISM OF OUR LORD FIRST SERMON

Except ye be born again of water and the Spirit, ye cannot enter the kingdom of God.

The season of Epiphany celebrates the manifestation of Christ as Son of God. He is the new wisdom manifested in the midst of the doctors in the Temple; he is the new power, manifest at Cana, transforming the dark waters of our humanity into the new and fiery wine of divine life in the Spirit, healing the leprosy and palsy of our sick nature. He is the new light, illuminating not only the ancient faith of Israel, but shining forth and summoning the kings and wise men of the East. He shines forth into all the world: 'Brightest and best of the sons of the morning' – the glory of Israel, and the light of the Gentiles.

In the early centuries of the Church, and still in Eastern Christendom, the event in which the Lord's epiphany was chiefly celebrated was his baptism by St John the Baptist, in which his mission is sealed by the visible descent of the Spirit, and the voice from heaven: 'Thou art my beloved son, in thee I am well pleased.' In parts of the Eastern Church especially, Epiphany is called the 'Feast of Lights', referring to the great array of torches and tapers with which the blessing of the waters is performed on this festival, symbolizing the spiritual illumination to which Jesus' baptism consecrates the element of water.

THE SOUL'S PILGRIMAGE

Water and fire: elements in contradiction; nature and spirit, humanity and divinity – he has brought them together, and has overcome the enmity, making them one. It is the sign of that new world, that new creation, in which we are made partakers of divinity, by God's sharing of our humanity. The ancient contradiction, the alienation, is broken down; for Christ is the epiphany, the manifestation, of 'God with us', Emmanuel; 'not by the conversion of the Godhead into flesh, but by the taking of manhood into God'. It is the sign of a new elevation, a new spiritual life.

How far this goes beyond the witness of John the Baptist is hard to imagine: so far that 'even the least in the kingdom of Heaven is greater than he.' John came preaching the baptism of repentance, his mind and heart fixed upon the hope and testimony of the prophets and martyrs of Israel. He heralded the dawn of the day of the Lord, a new era of justice and peace; and he knew that the new age must involve a radical change in the life of his people. Away with shams and hypocrisies: 'now is the axe laid to the root of the tree'; the crisis has come, the kingdom of God is at hand. He was 'the voice of one crying in the wilderness. Prepare ye the way of the Lord, make his paths straight.'

He knew little of what the inner life of that new kingdom might be. He was not the Messiah, nor even that new kingdom's prophet. But the water of his baptism was the outward sign of the necessary cleansing of the people's mind and will to prepare for the flaming gospel of Christ. 'I indeed baptize you with water; but there cometh one mightier than I ... he shall baptize you with the spirit and with fire.'

John was reluctant to baptize Jesus; but Jesus insisted upon identifying himself with this movement of purification:

BAPTISM OF OUR LORD FIRST SERMON

'thus it becometh us to fulfil all justice.' Thus he allied himself with the justice of the prophets and martyrs of the past. 'And straightway coming up out of the water,' illuminated in this act of humility, 'he saw the heavens rent asunder, and the Spirit as a dove descending upon him; and a voice came out of the heavens: "Thou art my beloved Son, in thee I am well pleased".'

Water and the Spirit: not only repentance and rectitude, not only a justice according to the law, not only a purification, however necessary and however radical, not only water, but the Spirit – a new elevation, a new inner attitude and motivation, a partaking of divinity.

Then 'immediately, Jesus was led by the Spirit into the wilderness,' and there this new spirituality was worked out in the course of his temptations: not bread first, however necessary and important; not bread first, but first the Word of God; not manipulation by spectacular tricks and gimmicks, but patience in the providence of God; not the outward kingdom of the external dominions of the earth, but the inner conquests of the truth. Not, perhaps, what John had imagined: something far more radical.

'Even the least in the kingdom of Heaven is greater than John the Baptist,' says Jesus. But how hardly do we understand that; how hard it is to see even as far as John's baptism of repentance. How easy to trust the bread and the gimmicks and the external powers; how hard to trust the Spirit's way of inner transformation. The Reformers must always remind the Church it is not our works that save us, whether they be the anxious churchly works which a Luther denounced, or the anxious worldly works which now so occupy our attention. Without the Spirit, they are dead.

Without the Spirit, the waters are dark and barren, a chaos,

THE SOUL'S PILGRIMAGE

and a senseless abyss of infinitely pointless activity. It is the Spirit from the opening heavens that makes them fruitful and seals our divine sonship. 'Among those born of woman, none is greater than John the Baptist,' says Jesus, 'yet even the least in God's kingdom is greater than he,' for 'that which is born of the flesh is flesh, and that which is born of the Spirit is spirit,' wherefore, 'except ye be born again of water and the Spirit, ye cannot enter the kingdom of God.'

In this liturgy which we celebrate, during the Offertory, there is a little ceremony which is not always noticed. A little water is mixed with the wine, and there is an ancient prayer for the priest to say as he does this: 'O God, who didst wonderfully create, and yet more wonderfully restore the dignity of human nature; grant that by this mystery of wine and water we may be made partakers of his divinity, who emptied himself to share our humanity.'

That is to say, our business here is not simply repentance and moral rectitude; that is no doubt a necessary preparation, but the kingdom of God is so much more than that. We are concerned with a new elevation of Spirit – 'God with us' – a whole new starting point of thought and action, a new spiritual life, a new birth.

That is what is manifest in the baptism of Jesus: let it now be manifest in us.

Amen.

BAPTISM OF OUR LORD SECOND SERMON

That which is born of the flesh is flesh; and that which is born of the Spirit is spirit.

Ever since the fourth century, certainly, and perhaps for a long time before that, the traditions of Eastern and Western Christendom in the celebration of Epiphany have been very different. In the West, it has been primarily the festival of the three kings: Christ the Son of God, manifest in infancy to the star-led sages of the gentiles. The East, on the other hand, has always kept Epiphany as a commemoration of the baptism of Christ by St John the Baptist: the manifestation of Christ's divine sonship by the visible descent of the Spirit upon him, and the voice from heaven, saying 'Thou art my beloved Son.'

The reasons for the difference are obscure. I have a suspicion (but, mind you, it's only a suspicion) that the West, resolutely orthodox through the great and terrible theological controversies of the fourth and fifth centuries, was nervous about emphasizing the baptism story, which had so often been used in support of the notion that the man Jesus became at that point the adopted Son of God, and preferred to emphasize instead the manifestation of divinity in the infant Christ, acknowledged by the Magi. However that may be, they are certainly quite different traditions.

THE SOUL'S PILGRIMAGE

Now, however, by virtue of our 1959 revision of the *Prayer Book*, in a spirit of ecumenical largess, we Canadian Anglicans are permitted to have it both ways, and so we have this extra festival; and, I trust, we will not be thereby tempted towards Adoptionism!

John the Baptizer came up from the wilderness of Judaea, 'clothed in camel's hair, and with a girdle of skins about his loins.' John, the fierce, uncompromising prophet, came preaching the baptism of repentance, his mind and heart fixed upon the hope and witness of all the prophets and martyrs of Israel, proclaiming the terrible 'Day of the Lord'. Away with shams and hypocrisies: 'Now is the axe laid to the root of the tree'; the crisis has come, 'the kingdom of God is at hand'. Repent. Be baptized. Bring forth fruits worthy of repentance.

He was not the Messiah, nor even that new kingdom's prophet, and perhaps he knew little of what that kingdom's inner life might be. But the water of his baptism represented a symbolic washing off of the guilty past, a symbolic cleansing of the people's mind and will, in preparation for the fiery gospel of the Lord. 'I indeed baptise you with water,' he says, 'but there cometh one mightier than I... he shall baptize you with the Spirit and with fire.'

Jesus insisted that he be baptized by John, for 'thus,' he says, 'it becometh us to fulfill all righteousness.' Thus he allies himself with the aspirations of the prophets and the law. The righteousness of his kingdom is not less, but more than that. 'And straightway coming up out of the water,' illumined in this act of humility, 'he saw the heavens opened, and the Spirit as a dove descending upon him; and a voice came from the heavens: "Thou art my beloved son, in thee I am well pleased".' This is not the moment of his adoption; rather, it is a moment of his

BAPTISM OF OUR LORD SECOND SERMON

epiphany – a moment of manifestation of what the Son of God, the Word of God, always is, but manifest now at a new level.

Here, there is revealed a new beginning; the manifestation of a new starting point, a new standpoint, which goes immeasurably beyond the vision of St John the Baptist. Water and the Spirit: not only repentance and the will towards rectitude; not just regrets and resolutions; not just the aspiration towards justice according to the law; not only water, but the Spirit's illumination – a new elevation of mind and heart, a partaking of divinity, which goes immeasurably beyond all possible regrets and resolutions.

The meaning of that new standpoint is marvellously illustrated in the story of Jesus' temptations, which follows immediately after the story of the baptism. Not bread, first, however necessary; but first the Word of God. Not the leap from the temple's pinnacle; not crafty tricks and gimmicks, but patience in the providence of God. Not the devil's kingdom of worldly domination, but the inner conquest of the truth. Not, perhaps, what John imagined, not deliverance from gentile overlords, and the struggle for purity according to the law, but something far more radical. John baptized in the wilderness, beyond Jordan; just beyond the border of the promised land: he sums up the old covenant of law, with its regrets and resolutions, and he stands just on the verge of the new covenant of grace. Therefore, says Jesus, 'even the least in the kingdom of heaven is greater than John the Baptist'.

But how hard that is to understand. How hard it is to cross that river. How hard it is to see even as far as John's baptism of repentance. How easy to trust the bread and the gimmicks, and the external powers; how hard to trust the Spirit's way of inner transformation. But we are not saved by bread and circuses. And

THE SOUL'S PILGRIMAGE

it is not our works that save us, whether they be the works of the ancient law, or the anxious churchly works denounced by the Reformers, or the anxious worldly works which so engage us and distract us nowadays. Nor are we saved by our regrets and resolutions. Without the Spirit, all these are dead, and worse than dead.

Without the Spirit, the waters are dark and barren: a chaos, a senseless abyss of infinitely pointless activity. It is the Spirit from the opening heavens which makes them fruitful, and seals our sonship. 'Among those born of woman,' says Jesus, 'none is greater than John the Baptist', 'yet even the least in the kingdom of heaven is greater than he'; 'for that which is born of the flesh is flesh, and that which is born of the spirit if spirit, wherefore ye must be born again.'

What Christ manifestly is by nature, the children of his kingdom are to be, by adoption and grace: partakers of divinity, beloved sons of God and heirs of life eternal. In this festival, we celebrate the Spirit's work: the new baptism of water and the Spirit, the holy nativity of the Word of God within our very souls, and the epiphany of that Word in all the world.

Let the heavens open, and let the Spirit descend upon the bitter waters of our humanity.

Amen.

EPIPHANY I

Be not conformed to this world, but be ye transformed
by the renewing of your mind, that ye may prove
what is that good, and acceptable,
and perfect will of God.

The season of Epiphany is all about the manifestation, the showing forth, the shining forth, the '*Epiphania*' of the divine glory in Jesus Christ, the eternal Son of God. And thus, all the commemorations which constitute this season are a continuing meditation upon the meaning and implications of the Christmas miracle: the miracle of God with us, God in our flesh, Emmanuel; the miracle of God visible to human eyes, God audible to human ears, God tangible to human touch; the miracle of God manifest in human life, restoring it and transforming it by the grace and truth he brings; that all may see what is the dispensation of the mystery, which from the beginning of the world had been hid in God, who created all things. The eternal Word, God of God, Light of Light, Very God of Very God, Jesus Christ, the eternal Son, was made flesh and dwelt among us, and we beheld his glory, the glory as of the only-begotten Son of God, full of grace and truth.

Epiphany is about that showing forth, that manifestation, and that beholding of glory, and it is also about the effects of that beholding: so that 'we all, with open face beholding as in a glass the glory of the Lord, are changed into the same image

THE SOUL'S PILGRIMAGE

from glory to glory even as by the Spirit of the Lord.' That is the essential theme of Epiphany: the manifestation of God's glory in Jesus Christ; our beholding of that glory, and the transforming power of that vision.

All the scripture lessons appointed for the festival and the Sundays following provide a logical explication of that essential theme. Thus, in the traditional lectionary of Western Christendom, which in this respect goes back at least as far as the fourth century, the season begins, on the festival itself, with the Gospel story of the coming of the wise men.

'Where is he that is born king of the Jews? For we have seen his star in the East, and are come to worship him.' The learned travellers (perhaps Chaldean mathematicians or astronomers – there are many legends; we don't really know for sure) came to Jerusalem, the Royal City; but they were directed further on, to the obscure village of Bethlehem. And it was a strange sort of king they found there: they found an infant, with Mary, his mother, and they fell down and worshipped him. There, at the manger, they offered their gifts: gold, acknowledging a king; incense, the symbol of God's presence; and myrrh, the ancient funeral spice, recognizing the mortal human nature of the Son of God, destined to suffer and to die in sacrifice for all humanity.

'They fell down and worshipped him.' By faith – really, by faith alone – they beheld the glory, and were changed thereby: they did not return the way they had come, but went back to their own country 'another way', transformed by adoration. You see, that's the theme: beholding the glory, and being transformed by that vision.

Now, on this first Sunday after Epiphany we begin a series of lessons which explicate that theme in detail, and the logic of that series is spelled out in today's collect:

EPIPHANY I

> O Lord, we beseech thee mercifully to receive the prayers of thy people which call upon thee; and grant that they may both perceive and know what things they ought to do, and also may have grace and power faithfully to fulfil the same; through Jesus Christ our Lord.

Notice the two aspects of that petition: first, 'that they may perceive and know'; secondly, 'that they may have grace and power faithfully to fulfil the same.' First, knowledge, then enabling grace; that's the order. Thus on this first Sunday after Epiphany, our Gospel lesson is about the epiphany of divine knowledge, divine wisdom, in the child Jesus, in the Temple at Jerusalem. On the following Sundays we have stories of the miracles – the symbolic acts of Jesus – illustrating the enabling and transforming power of divine grace; and in each case, the accompanying Epistle lesson makes a practical application to our own spiritual life.

Today's Gospel lesson, the story of Jesus' visit to the Temple, at the age of twelve, and his disputation with the learned doctors, is the only story the Gospels give us of the childhood of Jesus; and it's an interesting and remarkable story in many ways. But the essential point of it as the Gospel lesson for this Sunday is the manifestation of divine wisdom.

In the scriptures, especially in the Epistles of St Paul, the wisdom of God is often contrasted with the wisdom of the world, or the wisdom of the present age. 'Has not God made foolish the wisdom of the world? For since, in the wisdom of God, the world did not know God through wisdom, it pleased God through the folly of what we preach to save those who believe.' St Paul's point is that the wisdom of God, manifest in Christ, stands in contradiction to worldly wisdom, to all worldly calculation and expectation, in contradiction to all the schemes our cleverness would devise. The wisdom of God, in Christ, gives us a new knowledge, a new starting point; and our life as Christians must be radically dependent upon that revelation of divine wisdom. Therefore, says our Epistle lesson, 'Be not conformed to this world (i.e., to the wisdom of this present age), but be ye transformed by the renewing of your mind.'

The temptations to conformity are ever with us; the spirit of the age presses in upon us; the claims of expediency, of common sense, of majority opinion, and so on, seem often very strong indeed, and we find ourselves confused as to 'what is the good, and acceptable, and perfect will of God'.

But the message of Epiphany is all about that: the wisdom of God, the mystery hidden from the foundation of the world, is now manifest in Christ. 'For he has made known to us in all wisdom and insight the mystery of his will, according to his purpose which he set forth in Christ as a plan for the fulness of time, to unite all things in him, things in heaven and things on earth.'

And that wisdom is ours to believe, and to understand, and to make our own, by 'the renewing of our mind.' By faith beholding the glory, we are changed into the same image – transformed by adoration.

Here and now for us is Bethlehem. For here and now God in Christ is manifest to us in Word and Sacrament, in wisdom and gracious power. It is by beholding, by the habit of adoration, that we are changed. That is the basis of our spiritual life, and that is the meaning of Epiphany.

> Be not conformed to this world, but be ye transformed by the renewing of your mind …

Amen.

EPIPHANY II

*This beginning of signs did Jesus in Cana of Galilee,
and manifested forth his glory,
and his disciples believed on him.*

'Epiphany' is a Greek word meaning 'manifestation' – a showing forth, or shining forth – and what we celebrate in this Epiphany season is the shining forth of the glory of God in the Incarnation, in Jesus Christ, who is 'Light from Light'. From ancient times, the events most intimately associated with the festival are the baptism of Jesus – when the divine voice proclaims him to be the beloved son; and the coming of the wise men, or Magi, 'from eastern lands': 'Gentiles shall come to thy light, and kings to the brightness of thy rising.'

The Sundays after Epiphany continue this theme: the manifestation of God in Christ. On the first Sunday, it is the showing forth of divine wisdom in the disputation with the doctors in the temple; and the Gospel lessons for the following Sundays are a series of miracle stories: the changing of water into wine at the wedding feast of Cana; the cleansing of a leper; the healing of the centurion's servant; and the calming of the angry sea.

The point of these miracle stories in the Gospels, and the reason they are appointed for these Epiphany Sundays, is that they manifest the glory of God in Jesus Christ, 'the glory as of the only-begotten of the Father, full of grace and truth'.

THE SOUL'S PILGRIMAGE

These miracles are not the astonishing tricks of a magician. The world of Jesus' time was quite accustomed to magicians; perhaps you remember Simon the magician, from the Book of Acts, who wanted to buy the Holy Spirit to improve his magic. But the object of Jesus was not to achieve power by astonishing tricks; that was one of the rejected temptations. 'Cast yourself down from the pinnacle of the Temple,' said the devil 'you won't be hurt, because the angels will rescue you – you won't even stub your toe.'

Nor are the miracles of Jesus just a response to immediate human needs – to help the sick, the hungry, the bereaved, the embarrassed, the fearful. He could have turned stones into bread, so that no one need ever be hungry. But that is not the point of the miracles.

As St John's Gospel, in particular, makes clear, the miracles of Jesus are 'signs' – significant acts – signifying the nature of the doer. He feeds the hungry and signifies that he is the bread of life; he gives sight to the blind, and shows that he is the light of the world; he raises the dead, and shows that he is the resurrection and the life.

In today's Gospel lesson, we have the beginning of these signs at Cana of Galilee. The transformation of water into wine is the epiphany of Jesus as Lord of a new creation, by which his former work is to be exalted to a higher place and function in the dispensation of his providence. In this sign, he prefigures that work of re-creation, which – then and now – he causes to be wrought in his kingdom, for the salvation of souls and bodies. Simple elements pass silently beneath the power of his blessing: his servants bear forth, water becomes generous wine. So baptism exalts souls and bodies from the kingdom of nature to the kingdom of grace; and the Holy Eucharist is a means by which

EPIPHANY II

our nature is built up into the nature of Christ, 'changed from glory to glory'.

St Thomas Aquinas explains:

> Creation is a movement from nothingness into being. And this being is twofold: the being of nature and the being of grace. The first creation was established when God called creatures from nothing into the being of nature. Then creation was new, but it became old through human sin. It is fitting, therefore, that there should be a new creation, in which creatures should be established in the being of grace, which is a kind of creation from nothing; because whoever lacks grace is in fact nothing; and so it is clear that the gift of grace is a kind of creation.

The changing of water to wine is a sign of God's new creation, the transformation of nature and so it is the beginning of signs. It is the epiphany of God's power to make all things new, including particularly our human nature. 'For in Christ Jesus,' says St Paul, 'neither circumcision nor uncircumcision availeth anything, but a new creature.' And something of the character of our re-created nature is set forth in today's Epistle.

We are accustomed to think of nature as an order essentially fixed and unchangeable. Despite our technological and psychological manipulations, it seems essentially and endlessly the same thing. Particularly, our own human nature seems quite tiresomely unchangeable.

But by the power of God, by the grace of God, by the love of God, it has been changed, it is being changed, and it shall be changed; and that is the miracle of new creation. And day by day, that miracle goes on. Perhaps it is slow, and almost imperceptible; no doubt it seems often discouraging and painful; but the Lord of new creation is manifest in our midst, and his grace will have its triumph.

In the Offertory in the Eucharist, a little water is mixed with the wine, and there is an ancient prayer to accompany that ceremony:

> 'O God, who didst wonderfully create, and yet more wonderfully renew the dignity of human nature; grant that by this mystery of water and wine we may be partakers of his divinity, who emptied himself to share our humanity.'

Partakers of his divinity: that is the true miracle, of which the miracle at Cana is the sign. The bitter waters of our fallen humanity are to be sweetened by the grace of his divinity. That is the meaning of Epiphany: that we may see 'the glory of God in the face of Jesus Christ', and beholding that glory, may be 'transformed into that same image, from glory to glory'.

Amen.

EPIPHANY III

Be not wise in your own conceits.

If we consider the text of our Epistle lesson in the context of the whole twelfth chapter of Romans, including the Epistle lessons for the past two Sundays from the same chapter, we see that St Paul's point is not just a warning against self-satisfaction; it is also – and most importantly – an argument about the essential mutuality and reciprocity of wisdom. He is saying, 'Do not suppose that wisdom is your private possession, your individual achievement; do not think that you are wise just by yourself alone.' We have wisdom only as a common possession. We have many different gifts, just as 'in one body we have many members, and all members do not have the same function.' Genuine wisdom is a harmonic unity of differences.

One of the best illustrations I know of that point is Raphael's marvellous fresco of the 'School of Athens' in the papal apartments in the Vatican, a painting of which you may have noticed in several places around the university. In the first decade of the sixteenth century Pope Julius II, a powerful reforming pope, '*il papa terribile*', having laid the foundation stone for the new St Peter's Basilica, summoned a well-known Florentine sculptor, Michelangelo, to become a painter in the Sistine Chapel, and commissioned an unknown painter, Raphael, from Urbino, to redecorate the papal apartments. Julius wished to baptize the somewhat paganizing humanism of the Renaissance,

Raphael, Fresco, Apostolic Palace, Rome (1509-1511), 'The School of Athens'.

EPIPHANY III

and to show the essential unity and harmony of all ancient and Christian wisdom. In representing that magnificent conception, his young artists served him well.

In 'The School of Athens', Raphael depicts a remarkable assortment of people, lively groups of masters and students, some of them busy taking notes, all of them arranged on the steps of a great portico. In one corner is Euclid, measuring a diagram, attended by Zoroaster and Ptolemy, astronomers, playing with celestial globes. In another corner sits the mystic mathematician, Pythagoras, with Averroes looking over his shoulder at a chart of equivalents. And there, too, is Heraclitus (looking very much like Michelangelo), the very picture of the tortured poet, struggling for words. And so on.

At the apex of the assembly stand Plato and Aristotle, engaged in conversation, each clutching a book, surrounded by attentive students. Plato has a hand upraised, pointing to the heavens, while Aristotle has a hand outstretched, as though indicating the activity before him. People sometimes tell us that this means Plato is the idealist contrasted with Aristotle the empiricist. But that's a very modern notion and has nothing to do with Raphael and the Renaissance. The clue is rather to be seen in the books they carry. If you look very carefully, you can see the titles: Plato has the *Timaeus* and Aristotle has the *Ethics*. Thus they represent speculative and practical philosophy, not in opposition, but mutually complementary.

In all its harmonic diversity of subject and colour and form and motion, the picture stands for wisdom's unity in difference, for that mutuality and reciprocity in human life which the ancients knew as friendship, and which Christians know under its more universal and divine dimension as the grace of charity, without which, as St Paul explains, all our efforts are 'nothing worth'; not wisdom at all; just 'sounding brass and tinkling cymbal' – empty noise and nonsense. So, 'be not wise in your own conceits.'

But now, what does all that have to do with the season of Epiphany? Epiphany, as the word itself indicates, is all about the manifestation, the showing forth, the shining forth of the divine glory in Jesus Christ, the incarnate Son of God. 'The Word was made flesh and dwelt among us, and we beheld his glory, the glory as of the only-begotten of the Father, full of grace and truth.' Epiphany is about that showing, that manifestation, and that beholding of glory; and it is also about the effects of that beholding: so that 'we all, with open face beholding as in a glass the glory of the Lord, are changed into the same image from glory to glory, even as by the Spirit of the Lord'.

The wisdom of God, the mystery hidden from the foundation of the world is now manifest in Christ, and that wisdom is ours to behold, to believe, to understand, and to make our own, by the 'renewing of our mind'. By faith beholding the glory, we are changed into the same image – transformed by adoration. Here and now the glory of God in Christ is manifest in Word and sacrament, in wisdom and gracious power. It is by beholding, by the steady focusing of intellect and will, by the habit of adoration, that we are changed. That is the meaning of Epiphany, and that must be the basis of spiritual life in us.

So, 'Be not wise in your own conceits' but behold the glory and adore.

Amen.

CANDLEMAS
FIRST SERMON

Once ye were darkness, but now are ye light in the Lord.

Today we keep the feast of Candlemas, in which we celebrate the mystery of light. This commemoration of the Purification of St Mary, and the Presentation of her Son in the Temple at Jerusalem, is one of the most ancient Christian festivals, dating back at least to the fourth century, when the Church, freed from persecution, was first able to keep great festivals in public. And it is a feast of light, because it recalls the aged Simeon's inspired perception of Mary's son as old Israel's glory and the light of all persons universally.

The date is fixed, of course, by the prescription of the ancient Jewish law that the mother should be purified and the son presented forty days after the nativity; but there is also little doubt that the day was associated from the beginning with those ancient pagan festivals in which, after the darkness of the winter solstice, our remotest forebearers rejoiced in the sun's recovery of its strength, and the perceptible lengthening of the hours of light. Thus the festival combines the celebration of the cyclic, vacillating light of nature, and the dawning of the light of grace which knows no going down.

Given the vital properties of light – its illuminative and clarifying properties, its refining and generative influences – it

THE SOUL'S PILGRIMAGE

is hardly surprising that mankind from ancient times saw the light of nature as the symbol of divine glory and celebrated accordingly. Thus Plato spoke of the sun as the visible analogue of the divine good, the source of being and intelligibility, and Aristotle compared our halting perception of divine things to the feeble sight of bats, dazzled by the sun's light. And Julian the Apostate, the last of pagan Roman emperors, himself a Neoplatonist, striving to restore the spiritual life of Hellenistic paganism, fixed upon the cult of *Sol Invictus*, the Unconquerable Sun.

In the Bible, too, beginning with the Book of Genesis, light is everywhere the symbol of divine glory and divine revelation. In the narrative of creation, the first utterance of God – before the creation of the visible lamps of heaven – is *Fiat lux*, 'Let there be light.' And God saw the light, his first offspring, that it was good, and God separated the light from the darkness. And light is everywhere the symbol of divine guidance: the luminous cloud by day, and the pillar of fire by night, guide the wandering of his people through the wilderness. 'Thou, O God, shalt light my candle,' cries the psalmist: 'Thou, O Lord shalt make my darkness to be light.'

All that light – the light of nature and the light of prophecy – comes into focus in the festival we keep today; for today is a festival of the light of grace. Simeon hails the infant Christ as the light of Israel, and the light of all peoples everywhere, the clarifying of the types and shadows which are everywhere in nature, and everywhere in prophecy. This is therefore a festival of Incarnation and Epiphany, the shining forth of the Son of God. 'Light from Light', and we rejoice, as St Paul says, that 'God who commanded the light to shine out of darkness hath shined in our hearts, to give

CANDLEMAS FIRST SERMON

the light of the knowledge of the glory of God in the face of Jesus Christ.'

That is the general meaning of our festival of light; but we should also think about the more specific meaning of the Purification of Our Lady and the Presentation of her son. These are the ceremonies prescribed by the ancient law of Israel, which required that the first-born son must be redeemed – offered and bought back from God, the source of life and purity. With Jesus and his mother, the inner meaning of the ceremonial sacrifice is changed: the Son of God, who needs no redemption, and his mother, who lacks no purity, participate in an offering of perfectly free obedience, and make the offering of two turtle doves, which the law prescribes for the poor who cannot afford the sacrificial lamb.

This offering of the ritual sacrifice anticipates the more profound sacrifice of free obedience, when the Son himself will be the sacrificial lamb; for, as Simeon already sees, 'this child is set for the falling and rising again of many in Israel'. And Mary, too, will be drawn into this sacrifice: 'Yea, a sword shall pierce thy own soul also.' Thus what we have here is really a foreshadowing of the sacrifice of Christ, into which the Church is drawn, into which we ourselves are drawn, to die and rise again.

From that sacrifice, that freely lived obedience, shines forth the light of grace. Breaking forth from the night of the cross and his own people's rejection, shines forth the light of grace, its very core is the light of free obedience to the will of God. That is the light of truth which rises to clarify the confusion of our minds, to judge the darkness of our lives, and to enkindle the fire of charity in our hearts.

The light shines in the darkness, and the darkness does not

THE SOUL'S PILGRIMAGE

overcome it. It shines in the manifold darkness of greed and callowness, of pride and selfishness, and self-complacency and all the rest. 'If the light within you be darkness, how great is that darkness.'

But thank God, we are called out of darkness into light, 'once ye were darkness,' says St John, 'but now are ye light in the Lord' – walk then, in that light, walk as children of the light, walk in the light of sacrifice – the light of free obedience to the truth and charity of God.

That is the message of this festival of light, and that is always the meaning and message of this sacrament we celebrate: die and rise again, rejoice in the light – the light of nature and the light of grace, and the promise of the Gospel is that the light of nature and of grace will finally break forth in the light of glory, when the Son of Man shall come in final recapitulation, as the lighting which rises in the east and shines even to the west.

It seems that we have only earthbound offerings – only common bread and wine, but as Frederic Hölderlin reminds us, 'our bread is blessed by light, and the joy of wine comes from the thundering God.'

Once ye were darkness, but now are ye light in the Lord.

Amen.

CANDLEMAS
SECOND SERMON

For mine eyes have seen thy salvation.

Candlemas is a festival of light. As the seasons change, and the days lengthen, and the light returns to the world, we celebrate Christ as the world's true light. When we bless and light the candles, we symbolize that light, and symbolize, too, our vocation as bearers of that light.

By the law of ancient Israel, the first-born son was claimed for priestly service in the Temple at Jerusalem. Parents obtained their son's release from these duties by presenting him in the Temple, forty days after his birth, and paying a fee. In addition to the fee, an offering was expected, usually a lamb, but if the parents were too poor to afford a lamb, they might offer a pair of pigeons.

And so one day there came to the Temple a peasant family, seeking the redemption of the first-born. Mary, the young mother, was perhaps embarrassed that they could afford only the poor man's offering, but if so, her embarrassment must have turned to astonishment when Simeon, the aged servant of the Temple, took the baby in his arms, and hailed him as a Saviour of Israel, and the light of the Gentiles.

> Mine eyes have seen thy salvation, which thou hast prepared before the face of all people.

THE SOUL'S PILGRIMAGE

An astonishing speech it was — but its meaning was clear. The old man might now depart in peace, for he had lived on and on only in the inspired expectation that he should one day see the Lord's Christ. And surely it was only inspired expectation that could see the Lord's Christ in this child of poverty. 'Mine eyes have seen thy salvation.'

What does it mean to see God's salvation, except that we see very God himself. But, says St John, 'No man hath seen God at any time'. For God dwells in light inaccessible, beyond the farthest ranging of our senses, our imaginings and our reasonings. No man has seen God — yet the only begotten son has revealed him. In the mystery of the word made flesh, in the mystery of the Lord's Christ, 'We have touched and handled of the word of life.' As St Athanasius puts it, 'He was made man, that we might be made gods.'

But the Incarnation, the enfleshment of God in Christ is not a simple historical fact over and done with — something that we can recall and read about and wonder about — by the power of the Spirit, it is an ongoing reality in the life of the Body of Christ. And if we could see God in Christ, if we could see God's salvation, we must learn to see and love Christ now in one another. In fact, unless we can come to see Him in one another, I'm afraid we shall never come to see him at all. As St John says, 'He who loveth not his brother whom he hath seen, how can he love God whom he hath not seen?' 'And this commandment have we from him, that he that loveth God, love his brother also.'

We must learn to see him not only in the pious, the good, and the likeable, but perhaps especially in the lost, the troubled, the needy. 'In as much as ye have done it....' For in the mystery of his providence, 'God has chosen the weak things of this world

CANDLEMAS SECOND SERMON

to confound the strong, yea, and things which are not, to put to nought things which are'. All these are to be Christ-bearers for us, all these are lights in which we are to see God's salvation. Perhaps you know some who have been and are Christ-bearers for you – but their number is more vast, and their character more diverse, than one can easily imagine.

Conversely, and perhaps more difficult still, we ourselves are to be Christ-bearers to others, we are to be lights in which God's salvation may be seen. I'm sure you will allow that that is the role of the saints, but surely for most of us, it seems rather unlikely, and perhaps even rather presumptuous. Perhaps we're not very good at loving one another. So often we are stupid, and say and do the wrong things, and seem to do more harm than good. But 'God has chosen the weak things of the world to confound the strong' and his grace works as much in our weakness as in our strength.

Theologians commonly distinguish between sanctifying grace and gratuitous grace. Sanctifying grace is God's power working in us to transform our own nature; gratuitous grace is God's power working through us for others.

That grace which we have for others is not a function of our own virtue and sanctity: even in our confusion and doubt and weakness; even in our temptation and sinning, the gratuitous grace of God will have its way. It is the sign of God's power that he brings good even from our evil. Our blindness, our stupidity and even our sheer perversity are never outside his providence.

Therefore, neither rejoice in your strength and goodness, nor despair in your weakness and sin. Rejoice rather in the mystery of God's grace which overcomes and uses both – in ways past finding out.

He reveals his salvation in the poor infant of forty days. He makes weakness strength and strength weakness. He it is who makes all from nothing and life from death. He it is who turns water into wine, and he it is who now makes an insignificant bit of bread to be his glorious body. Therefore, rejoice in him.

'Mine eyes have seen thy salvation.'

Amen.

EPIPHANY V

And above all these things put on charity,
which is the bond of perfectness.

This is hardly the season for much activity in the garden, but it is perhaps the season for perusing the seed catalogues and considering what you'd like to see in your garden next summer. Most gardeners, I think, take pleasure in a neat and tidy garden: the carrots growing in straight rows, like soldiers on parade, the tomato plants neatly pruned and staked, and so on; and above all, not a weed in sight. We certainly won't plant any weeds.

But, alas, weeds are insidious, and diabolically clever. They sneak in somehow, and contrive to disguise themselves among the plants, and before you know it, they've reached such proportions that you really can't remove them without destroying the plants. Sometimes kind friends offer to help me with the weeding, but I must confess to sharing the reservations of the farmer in our Gospel lesson: it's a hazardous operation, and maybe it's impossible to remove the weeds without severe damage to the plants. Perhaps it's really best to let them grow together until harvest time. Today's parable is good advice for compulsive weeders, and if you should visit my garden in the summer, you would note that it's advice I take very much to heart.

But of course, the parable is not really about gardens, it's about people, about the mixture of good and evil in human life and human community, and about God's judgement. God is the farmer, who instructs his servants to be patient with the weeds, lest in their zeal to eradicate the weeds, they destroy the wheat as well. The separation of the tares from the wheat must wait until the harvest; that is to say, it must wait upon God's judgement.

Therefore, God's servants must not be hasty in judgement and condemnation; rather, as St Paul says in the Epistle lesson, they must put on 'mercy and compassion, kindness, humbleness of mind, meekness, long-suffering, forbearing one another and forgiving one another, if any have a complaint against any, even as the Lord forgave you, so also do ye.' God, thank God, is not a compulsive weeder, and we had better beware of trying to usurp his judgement. As Dante puts it in the *Paradiso*:

> Let no one be too self-assured
> In judging early, as one who would count the rows
> Of green blades in the field ere they matured
> For I have seen how first the wild-briar shows
> Her sprays, all winter through, thorny and stark
> And then upon the topmost bears the rose.

'And above all these things,' says St Paul, 'put on charity, which is the bond of perfectness', for it is only thus that the Church, God's household, as our Collect says, is kept in true religion. The point is clear and simple, and need not be belaboured here, and I think the practical applications of it in our relationships with one another are obvious enough if we are willing to see them.

The season of Epiphany is longer or shorter, depending upon the date of Easter, and this year this fifth Sunday is the

EPIPHANY V

end of the season. The essential message of the whole season is an explication of the meaning of God's Incarnation. Thus the Gospel lessons are all about the manifestation of divine wisdom and divine power in Jesus Christ – divine wisdom and divine power miraculously transforming human life and human community. The Epistle lessons always present some aspect of that transformation, some aspect of divine life manifest in our life; and today's lesson sums all that up in the terms of the divine gift of charity.

'And above all these things put on charity, which is the bond of perfectness', for that is the epiphany of divine life in us.

Amen.

SEPTUAGESIMA
FIRST SERMON

Know ye not that they which run in a race run all,
but one receiveth the prize?
So run that ye may obtain.

Today's liturgy, with its special Collect, Epistle and Gospel, marks an important turning point in the Christian year. Students of liturgy would say that we have now completed the Christmas cycle – that is, Advent, Christmas, and Epiphany – and we begin the Easter cycle – Lent, Holy Week, Easter, Ascension, and Pentecost.

Let's think for a moment about the meaning of those cycles.

In the weeks since the beginning of Advent, all our Collects, Epistles and Gospels, have centred around one theme: the expectation, the coming and the manifestation – the epiphany – of God, the Son of God, in our midst – the Word of God made flesh, full of grace and truth, manifest in wisdom and manifest in power. Now, in this second cycle, which begins today, we turn our minds to consider God's work for our salvation in Jesus Christ – his ministry, his suffering and sacrifice, his triumph in Easter and Ascension. And his sending of the Holy Spirit. So, the first cycle is about God's coming among us in Jesus Christ; the second is about his work for our salvation.

The three Sundays with Latin names – Septuagesima,

SEPTUAGESIMA FIRST SERMON

Sexagesima, and Quinquagesima – are really meant to constitute our preparation for that second cycle, and the scripture lessons for today should be thought about in that context. Perhaps it will help if we think first for a moment about the history of the selection of these particular lessons.

The 'Lectionary,' as it's called – the selection of lessons we read Sunday by Sunday at the Eucharist – is actually very ancient. In the form in which we have it in the *Prayer Book*, it goes back with very few alterations, well over a thousand years – much of it, including today's lesson, is much older than that, and goes back to early Christian times – and it was, until the second half of the twentieth century, the more or less common lectionary of the whole of Western Christendom.

However, whether or not we use the ancient common lectionary, there are perhaps still some things to be learned from thinking about its history and its rationale which seem to have been largely forgotten. For instance, one might recall that at one time in the early days of the Church, Septuagesima was actually the beginning of Lent, the day on which catechumens – new converts to Christianity – were first in church to begin their preparation for baptism at Easter. Think what today's lessons must have meant for them.

In the Epistle lesson, from St Paul's first Epistle to the Corinthians, they were reminded of the discipline which Christian life involves. Like those athletes in the Isthmian games in that great marble stadium near Corinth, they must direct all their energies towards attaining the prize – not a crown of wilting laurel leaves, but the imperishable crown of eternal life. They must not run erratically, nor waste their energies beating against thin air – they must become disciplined athletes of God.

Then the Gospel lesson, about the labourers called at various times to the vineyard. 'They received every one a penny.' Those who came at the last, eleventh hour received the same as those who had borne the burden and heat of the day. Well, just think of that early Christian congregation, which no doubt included many who had indeed borne the burden and heat of the day; many for whom their Christian profession had not been easy. Perhaps some of them had even been tortured in persecution. They were reminded that the reward of these newcomers – these catechumens – must be the same as theirs. And everyone was reminded that salvation is finally, at the end of the day, not something they have earned – for all their struggle; it is finally God's gracious gift, which they can only accept with thankful humility.

Well, conditions have changed. Lent does not begin today (we have two more weeks of preparation – and excellent preparation it is if we really think about its meaning) and we do not have the catechumens here preparing for Easter baptism. But the lectionary has not changed. We still have these same lessons, and the Church wisely retained them, because they are the ideal first step in the preparation of our minds for Lent and for what follows Lent. They insist upon two essential points, as relevant today as ever they were.

The first is this: Christian life is a life of discipline – discipline of mind, discipline of heart, discipline of will. We must train ourselves and shape our lives in ways consonant with our calling: in humility, in thankfulness, in charity, in temperance, and so on; mindful of our goal. We dare not run erratically, nor waste our time and energy beating empty air. We must concentrate on our task – that is what the discipline of Lent is all about.

And the second point is this: for all our labour and struggle, we do not earn salvation. Salvation is the free gift of God's mercy

SEPTUAGESIMA FIRST SERMON

and his grace. It is God who calls us to the vineyard, perhaps at the last, eleventh hour, and the prize is his free and generous gift. The master of the vineyard asks: 'Is it not lawful for me to do as I will with what is my own?' It is indeed his own, won by him in the saving work of Jesus Christ, and is ours only by faith in him. We have not earned it.

It seems to me that nothing could be more relevant than these two points – our discipline and God's free gift of salvation – as we prepare ourselves for Lent. But before I finish, I want to broaden the relevance of these two points just a bit.

I suppose there is no one here today whose mind is not occupied with the current state of world affairs, especially the crisis in the Persian Gulf – the misery already caused, and the possibility of more miseries to come. What do our lessons have to say about that? First, the point about discipline, the Epistle lesson, the discipline of mind and heart and will. There is nothing truly evil in this world which is not the fruit of ill-will; that is to say, of greed, or lust, or envy, or pride, or bigotry, and so on, and in that ill-will, we all have part, however insignificant it may seem. We are called to shape our own lives in the ways of charity and justice, and, so far as we are able, to influence the lives of others, in our own families, and communities, and nations, and internationally, in those same virtues. That is at the heart of our struggle: the discipline of will. 'I keep under my body', says St Paul, and that's exactly what he means – the discipline of will.

The second point, the Gospel lesson, is this: The prize is God's free gift. God's providence rules all, and that providence, however hidden from us may be its ways, is always good, and always present: 'not a sparrow falleth without your heavenly Father.' He upholds all things by the work of his power. And so we run the race, not uncertainly, but in the sure confidence, the

THE SOUL'S PILGRIMAGE

faith, that all things, all things – even the ugly, horrid things – work together for Good to those who love God.

Therefore, says St Paul, 'So run that ye may obtain.'

Amen.

SEPTUAGESIMA
SECOND SERMON

Why stand ye here all the day idle?

The calendar of the Christian year seems to divide things in a somewhat artificial way: at one time we celebrate the nativity of Christ; at another time we recall his Passion; then we celebrate his resurrection; and then we give thanks for the inspiration of God's Pentecostal Spirit, and so on. Somewhat artificial, I say, because really the Christian religion requires that we be mindful of all these things at once. Just as historically the nativity of Christ finds its fulness of meaning only in his Passion and resurrection, so in our practice of religion, the birth of divine life in our souls is realized only through suffering and exaltation, and our elevation to a new level of life in the Spirit. All these things belong together; they are parts of a whole and make sense only in terms of that whole.

Yet we are creatures of time and place, and circumstance, and we have to divide these things – we cannot see them in one simple glance. If we try to see and celebrate everything at once, we end up seeing and celebrating nothing at all. We must see one thing, and then another; we suffer on one day, and rejoice on another. 'Heaviness may abide for a night but joy cometh in the morning.' It is the great genius of the Christian calendar that it shows us all these things, piece by piece; in an orderly and coherent way. One

THE SOUL'S PILGRIMAGE

thing is connected with another, so that in the course of a whole year, if we follow it carefully, we are presented with the whole of Christian faith and practice in a coherent form and shown the pattern of our spiritual life in all its wholeness.

Most of us, and even our greatest spiritual leaders, are inclined to see things in one-sided ways; we tend to have special interests and enthusiasms, and we are inclined to emphasize one thing, and to neglect the rest as unimportant. The discipline of the Christian calendar recalls us to balance and objectivity.

The Church year, as we observe it, has remained practically unchanged since the early centuries of Christianity, and the lessons from the scriptures which we read each Sunday are, by and large, those which were read in Christian churches fifteen or sixteen centuries ago. There is much interest just now in the revision of the calendar and the lessons; but I hope that we will be very cautious about that, lest we finish by rashly substituting our own momentary fancies and enthusiasms for the integrity of the Christian faith. The ancient calendar is a work of great spiritual genius, and its scripture lessons are prescribed with superb logic and profound insight.

Today we begin a series of three Sundays which are preparatory to Lent – Septuagesima, Sexagesima, and Quinquagesima. The names of the Sundays are the old Latin names, meaning the seventieth, sixtieth and fiftieth days (approximately) before Easter. The names are not particularly important; but what the message of these Sundays tells us about Lent, and about the nature and development of our spiritual life, is profoundly important. Obviously, I mustn't try to explain the scriptures for all three Sundays this morning; but I do want to say, very briefly, what their message is, and then add a few more detailed remarks about today's Epistle and Gospel lessons.

The message of the preparatory Sundays represents Lent

SEPTUAGESIMA SECOND SERMON

as a journey and a labour. We are like athletes, striving for the mastery, to attain the incorruptible crown of God's kingdom. We labour in the vineyard, for the reward which God's free grace provides. Next Sunday's Gospel reminds us that the seed of God's Word is sown in our hearts, and we must not let it be choked by the thorns of worldly preoccupations; the Epistle tells us of the hardships and infirmities that attend its growth. On Quinquagesima, the Gospel sets all this in the context of Christ's journey to Jerusalem to die and rise again, healing, by his charity, the blind man by the wayside; and the Epistle tells us that that 'more excellent way' of charity must be the character of our own journey, for without that, all our labours are 'nothing worth'. Thus Lent is to be an exercise in growth to spiritual maturity – a putting off of 'childish things' – a struggle to follow our saviour through suffering to risen life.

That is, of course, a description of the whole of our life as Christians; but we must have times of special emphasis, and Lent is to be a time of special emphasis upon the disciplines of that journey. St Paul, in today's Epistle, sets the tone: writing to the Corinthians, he reminds them of the great athletic contests with which they were familiar. 'Know ye not that they which run in a race run all, but one receiveth the prize? So run that ye may obtain.' Not as runners who are uncertain of their course, nor as fighters who aimlessly beat against thin air. This lesson from St Paul must have had particular significance in the ancient Church for the new converts, who were normally in Church for the first time on Septuagesima, beginning their preparation for baptism at Easter; but the message is certainly relevant for us all: train and discipline yourself, don't be vague and aimless, take the practical measures necessary to the spiritual end you seek.

The Gospel lesson, too, must have seemed especially

THE SOUL'S PILGRIMAGE

significant to the new converts, when it speaks of those who have come at the eleventh hour to labour in the vineyard. There is one prize; there is one reward: 'they received every one a penny.' There is one kingdom of God, and it is the life of that kingdom that all of them receive. 'Early in the morning' or at the 'eleventh hour'; it is never too early or too late to labour for that kingdom: 'Behold now is the accepted time, now is the day of salvation.' 'Why stand ye here all the day idle? Go ye also into the vineyard, and whatsoever is right, that shall ye receive.' And the reward is not according to worldly merit, but according to God's own grace: 'I will give unto this last even as unto thee.'

The Gospel lesson closes with a very solemn warning: 'many be called, but few chosen.' St Gregory the Great, preaching on this Sunday fourteen centuries ago, said this:

> Many keep company with God in word, but shun him in deed … And within the Church, dearest brethren, you will see many such persons, but you must neither imitate them nor despair of them. What a man is today, you can see, but what each will be tomorrow, no one knows … Two things there are therefore upon which we should carefully reflect. Because many are called and few chosen, the first is: let no one presume on his own salvation; for though he be called to faith, whether he is worthy of the eternal kingdom he knows not. The second is: let no one presume to despair of his neighbour, whom perhaps he sees lying in sin; for he knows not the riches of the divine mercy.

'Why stand ye here all the day idle? Go ye also into the vineyard, and whatsoever is right, that shall ye receive.'

Amen.

SEPTUAGESIMA
THIRD SERMON

*Go ye also into the vineyard,
and whatsoever is right,
that shall ye receive.*

In the seasons of Christmas and Epiphany, we celebrate the Word made flesh, the Word of God, the truth of God, made manifest in the world in the humanity of Jesus Christ. The divine wisdom, the eternal power and love of God, are shown to us, made manifest to us, in Jesus Christ, proclaimed in signs and wonders. The Word is made flesh, God is manifest in Christ, that we might behold his glory, 'full of grace and truth', that we might know the wisdom, power and love of God; that we might share in heart and mind the life of God himself as an ancient prayer puts it, 'that we might be made partakers of his divinity, who emptied himself to share our humanity'. That is the meaning of Epiphany, the Word of God is manifest, the truth of God is shown to us, so that our lives might be changed – 'not conformed to the present age, but transformed by the renewing of our minds'.

Now, as we approach the Lenten season, we consider more fully the nature of that transformation. Lent is about conflict and suffering, about death and resurrection. It is about Jesus' resurrection, certainly; but also about our own, as we follow his road, through conflict and temptation, to Jerusalem. Our transformation, the renewing of our minds in conformity to the Word of God, is a kind of dying and rebirth – it is death to an old nature, an old worldliness, an old conformity to this present age, which does not give up without a struggle. As St Augustine says in his *Confessions*: 'Those trifles of all trifles, those vanities of vanities ... held me back, plucking at the garment of my flesh, softly murmuring, "Are you sending us away? From this moment, shall we not be with you, now or ever?"' Those old, long-cherished demons will not be easily dismissed; they will be cast out only by much prayer and fasting. That is the meaning of the disciplines of Lent.

But between Epiphany and Lent, there are three Sundays, with ancient Latin names: Septuagesima, Sexagesima, and Quinquagesima – the seventieth, sixtieth, and fiftieth days, approximately, before Easter. And the intention of these three pre-Lenten Sundays is to prepare us for the journey and the labour, the pilgrimage of Lent. Thus St Paul reminds us in today's Epistle, we are to be like athletes, competing in a struggle, athletes in training, temperate in all things; not aimless, but disciplined, striving for a prize which is immortal. The Gospel likens us to workers in a vineyard. It matters not whether we come early in the morning, or at midday, or at the last, eleventh hour: 'Ye labour for the one reward which God's free grace provides.' Whether the hour be late or early matters not; the point is that now we are called to spiritual reward, and now we must give up our idleness.

Next Sunday's Gospel will remind us that the seed of God's Word has been planted in our hearts, and that we must not let it perish by the drought of our neglect, nor let it be stolen by the devil's wiles, nor choked by thorns of worldly preoccupations. And the Epistle will speak to us of the hardships and infirmities which attend the nurture of that plant. 'In labours more abundant; in stripes above measure; in prisons more frequent; in deaths

SEPTUAGESIMA THIRD SERMON

oft.' On Quinquagesima, the Gospel lesson will set all this in the context of Christ's journey to Jerusalem, to die and rise again, healing, by his charity the blind man by the wayside; and the Epistle will tell us that the 'more excellent way' of charity must be the character of our own journey, for without that, all our labours will be 'nothing worth' – just 'sounding brass or tinkling cymbal'. Thus these preparatory Sundays introduce Lent as a journey, a pilgrimage, a labour, an exercise in growth to spiritual maturity, a putting off of 'childish things' – a struggle to follow Christ through suffering to risen life.

But this journey and this labour, this pilgrimage to spiritual maturity, what can it mean for us? What is this transformation, this 'renewal of the mind' which rejects the present age and conforms us to the manifested Word of God? Lent comes and goes – year after year, and perhaps it doesn't seem to make much difference, really – no great spiritual enlightenment, no great victories over the demons which so persistently beset us. Trifles and vanities still clutch our garments and hold us back. As the poet says, 'the world is too much with us; late and soon, getting and spending, we lay waste our powers.'

Our own society in this present age is no doubt the most affluent the world has ever known. Yet it is also a world of the most abject spiritual poverty, and aimless, frustrated, wasted lives. There is certainly a hunger for the Spirit's goods, vigorously, if superficially, exploited by hucksters of the Word of God. Everywhere there is talk of 'spirituality,' and Churches do surveys and form committees to promote it. But all too often they speak as though spirituality were some sort of hobby, a kind of option, some luxury, which people who are bored with life might now take up, some fine embroidery upon the cloth of worldliness for those who have a taste for it. But spirituality is not a hobby; it is not something added on; our real

THE SOUL'S PILGRIMAGE

spirituality is the whole character of our life as human beings. Our real spirituality is the whole attitude and set of mind with which we wash our dishes, or drive our cars, or buy our shoes, or cast our votes, or play our games; it is the whole character and quality of our relations with our families and friends and enemies and neighbours. Spirituality is not necessarily Christian spirituality: there is certainly a spirituality of worldliness — that is precisely what St Paul refers to as conformity to this present age. It is that attitude, that set of mind which lives to feed the beast within us — that many-headed Hydra of whims, desires and appetites — with the manifold fads and fantasies which every day seduce us. And, indeed, individually and socially, we reap the consequences of such a spirituality, in hopelessly chaotic and frustrated lives: for no amount of bread and circuses, no amount of 'meat that perisheth' will ever satiate that beast. And meanwhile, the deepest hunger of the spirit is never even recognized. As today's collect so aptly puts it, we are 'justly punished for our offenses'.

Christian spirituality is a journey and a struggle: a struggle to wean ourselves from worldliness, to attain a liberty of spirit which is not subservient to whims and appetites and vain imaginations, but, rather, weighs and judges all things by the Word of God made manifest in Jesus Christ. Today's lessons challenge us to undertake afresh that transformation, that liberation and renewal of the mind, with disciplined attention; not as runners uncertain of the course, and not as fighters who strike randomly against thin air. By God's Word, by God's grace, we are called to labour earnestly in the vineyard of the spirit, now, even though it be the eleventh hour.

'Go ye also into the vineyard, and whatsoever is right, that shall ye receive.'

Amen.

SEXAGESIMA

*But that on the good ground are they which
in an honest and good heart, having heard the Word,
keep it, and bring forth fruit with patience.*

From the earliest times of Christianity, Lent has been observed as a forty-day period of fasting, in preparation for Easter: a forty-day fast in imitation of Jesus' fasting in the wilderness. But in various times and places, the forty days have been calculated in different ways, sometimes excluding Sundays, Thursdays, and Saturdays, sometimes excluding one or two of those days from the penitential season. Our present system of beginning Lent on Ash Wednesday has been constant since the time of St Gregory the Great, in the sixth century, and provides exactly forty fasting days, excluding the Sundays. But the three Sundays before Ash Wednesday – Septuagesima, Sexagesima, and Quinquagesima – were all at some time dates for the beginning of Lent, and the lessons for these Sundays still retain a Lenten character.

In our present usage, these three Sundays form a kind of introduction to Lent, a preparation of our minds and hearts for the labours and disciplines of Lent. Thus last Sunday's Epistle lesson spoke to us of the Christian life on the analogy of an athletic contest, in which the participants train themselves with careful discipline. 'Now they do it to obtain a corruptible crown,' says St Paul, 'but we an incorruptible' – the incorruptible crown of spiritual good. And then the Gospel lesson was Jesus' parable

THE SOUL'S PILGRIMAGE

of the labourers in the vineyard reminding us of the labours and the reward of God's eternal kingdom. It matters not whether we have come early in the morning, or at midday, or just now, at the last, eleventh, hour: we labour for the same reward, which God's free grace provides. 'Go ye also into the vineyard, and whatsoever is right, that shall ye receive.'

Today's Epistle lesson, from second Corinthians, continues that theme, and St Paul speaks of his 'labours more abundant', and challenges the pride and complacency of the Corinthians. If anyone has cause for boasting, surely his claims are better than most; but he knows the folly of all such glory. 'If I must needs glory,' he says, 'I will glory of the things which concern mine infirmities.' However great the trial we sustain in the labours of God's kingdom, the good that comes of them is of the Lord, and not of us, and his must be the glory.

Then the Gospel for today tells us how the kingdom is God's own planting. The seed is the Word of God, sown in our hearts, and we must not let it perish by the shallowness and drought of our neglect, nor let it be stolen by the devil's wiles, nor choked by thorns of worldly cares and busyness. Our care and labour must be for the cultivation of that planting. With an honest and good heart, we must keep the Word of God, and 'bring forth fruit with patience'.

All these lessons have a common emphasis: they speak of discipline, and labour, and watchful care; they speak of the struggle for spiritual maturity. It is that struggle that we are called to undertake, for the salvation of our souls. Certainly the kingdom is God's free gift, in Jesus Christ: the Word of God is manifest, the kingdom of God is in our midst, within our grasp.

In Jesus Christ, the secrets of that kingdom are unlocked, and the way is open. He is himself, 'the way, the truth, and the

SEXAGESIMA

life', and in him is full and free salvation. Certainly the kingdom is God's free gift, and yet, for us, it is a struggle and a labour, because it involves a transformation of ourselves, and for most of us, I think, that is a long and painful process. And, like the seed in Jesus' parable, it must be tended with watchful care.

I know there are many Christians now who speak of salvation as though it were some sort of instant remedy, an emotional experience which makes you feel good inside; and they sometimes speak of the doctrines and disciplines of traditional Christianity as unnecessary complications. But the life of the spirit is more than emotional experience, something more than feeling good inside. The life of God's kingdom involves a re-orientation of thought and will, a renewal of the mind, to see ourselves and our world in new perspective. Training ourselves in that perspective is a matter of labour and discipline, a matter of ongoing intellectual and moral effort.

Spiritual maturity is not a matter of quickly grasping a slate of instant easy answers. The answers are there, in the Word of God, the answers are illustrated in many ways in the lives of saints, in the wisdom of two thousand years of Christian life and thought. But for us, those answers are not easy, because of what we are. We must tune our jaded ears to hear the Word of God, we must train our feeble eyes to see the light – 'the light of the knowledge of the glory of God in the face of Jesus Christ'. No doubt the treasure is there for those who seek, and the door is open to those who knock, but the seeking and the knocking require heart and soul and mind and strength.

These three Pre-Lenten Sundays are a preparation for the spiritual exercises of Lent, and it's not too soon to be thinking about what each of us might undertake this year for the good of our immortal souls; what extra we might undertake by way

THE SOUL'S PILGRIMAGE

of intellectual and devotional exercise, what works of charity might be within our reach, what sins might be overcome. Lent is a time of spiritual discipline, and surely there is not one of us here who does not need its opportunities. Most of us, I'm sure, are very busy; but perhaps it is the busiest of us who most need those opportunities.

Let's all think carefully about the message of the Gospel for today. The Word of God has been sown in our hearts and must take root and grow there:

> Now the parable is this: The seed is the Word of God. Those by the wayside are they that hear; then cometh the devil, and taketh away the Word out of their hearts, lest they should believe, and be saved. They on the rock are they which, when they hear, receive the Word with joy; and these have no root, which for a while believe, and in time of temptation fall away. And that which fell among thorns are they which, when they have heard, go forth, and are choked with cares, and riches, and pleasures of this life, and bring no fruit to perfection. But that on the good ground are they which in an honest and good heart, having heard the Word, keep it, and bring forth fruit with patience.

The Word of God has been sown in our hearts. Having heard the Word, let us keep it, 'and bring forth fruit with patience'.

Amen.

QUINQUAGESIMA

Behold we go up to Jerusalem.

In the Gospel for today, Jesus announces his final journey to Jerusalem: 'Behold, we go up to Jerusalem,' he says, 'and all things that are written by the prophets concerning the Son of Man shall be accomplished.' He must die and rise again. 'Behold, we go up to Jerusalem.' That is what Lent is all about: we go up with him to Jerusalem, to gaze upon and share in his Passion, to be healed and transformed by that vision of the divine love. Perhaps you remember that peculiar story in the Book of Numbers, in which the Lord commands Moses to make a brazen serpent and set it up on a pole; 'and if a serpent bit any one, he would look at the bronze serpent and live'. According to St John's Gospel, Jesus took that image to himself: 'As Moses lifted up the serpent in the wilderness, even so must the Son of Man be lifted up, that whosoever believeth in him might have eternal life.' The Son of Man is to be lifted up on the cross. We are to gaze upon his Passion, and in that vision of sacrificial love, our wounded souls are to find healing and new life.

'And the disciples understood none of these things,' says today's Gospel. They, and also we ourselves, perhaps, are like that man at Jericho. We sit by the wayside begging, and we can't see what's going on here, what it's all about. 'They told him that Jesus of Nazareth passeth by.' The reason of this journey, the meaning of Jesus and his sacrifice, is perhaps not very clear to us. To journey with him is to journey in faith: 'Lord, that I may receive my sight.' Vision is the reward of faith.

Our journey to Jerusalem, our Lent, is to be a journey into light, a journey into understanding the mystery of divine love in the Passion of Christ. Can the lessons and the disciplines of Lent really do that for us? Certainly, that seems far-fetched, but then, that is the way of faith. God gives much in return for little; he gives all in return for nothing. All in return for nothing: that is the divine charity which, as St Paul explains in today's Epistle, is to be the very essence of our life as Christians. Faith is an excellent thing, no doubt, and so is hope, but they are only a beginning. In heaven there is no faith; in heaven there is no hope because heaven is the knowledge and possession of that eternal good, towards which faith and hope can only aim. In heaven there is only charity, the bond of love which unites lover and beloved. Without that love, all our powers are worthless: 'sounding brass and tinkling cymbal', or noisy nonsense. With the best gift of charity, we have eternal life. 'For what shall separate us from the love of Christ?'

Therefore, our journey of Lent is not just a journey of faith and hope, but a journey of love, a journey whereby we become more firm in that bond of love which unites us to God. It is a journey whereby we grow up in love. 'When I was a child, I spake as a child,' says St Paul. We are like children who babble aimlessly. Lent is a time to grow up and put away childish things.

The disciplines of Lent are a serious matter, being fundamentally a matter of the nourishment of our childish souls. I suppose that no age has ever been so diet-conscious as our own. Almost everyone looks at the package to see what noxious additives lurk within. But what thought do we take for spiritual nutriment? Wouldn't it be a good idea to try to wean ourselves

QUINQUAGESIMA

a little bit from the poisonous sweets of self-indulgence and worldly preoccupation? Sometimes children imagine that they could eat sweets exclusively forever. 'But when I became a man, I put away childish things.' Wouldn't we be better off with a little more time for prayer, and a little less for empty chatter, a little more time for the Word of God and a little less for trivial words? Habits are formed by disciplines; and the habit of charity, the habit of heaven, is not formed by self-indulgence, and the endless pursuit of worldly ends. 'Where your treasure is, there will your heart be also.' There is one pearl of great price, and, like the merchant in the parable, we may have to sell quite a lot to buy it.

Jesus bids us to go up with him to Jerusalem, and to find our treasure there. May he open our blind eyes and give us grace to do just that.

Amen.

ASH WEDNESDAY

Where your treasure is, there will your heart be also.

'Behold, we go up to Jerusalem,' said Jesus to his disciples in last Sunday's Gospel lesson.

'Behold, we go up to Jerusalem': that is the essential theme out of Lenten season. We are to go to Jerusalem with Jesus, to witness there the fulfilment of the ancient prophecies; to witness his death and resurrection; to witness the dying and the rising of the Son of God, for us and for our salvation. What we witness there is something God has done for us, once and for all: God the Son has borne our sins, in his own body, on the tree, and has won for us forgiveness and new life.

That is what God has done for us. It is something finished, sufficient and complete, never to be done again. God's infinite charity has done for us what we could never do. He has given us, each one, new life, liberty, a new beginning. That is something we could never do – it is the free gift of God's charity, 'for God so loved the world' . . . It is the free gift of God's charity, which we can only thankfully receive. That is what we call 'justification'.

'Behold, we go up to Jerusalem', to witness there what the charity of God has done for us, our justification. But what we witness in Jerusalem is not only what God in Christ has done for us, it is also something that must be done in us, day by day. Our justification must be the basis of our sanctification; and

ASH WEDNESDAY

that is what the spiritual labour of Lent is all about. Looking upon the crucified, we must learn to die and rise again, day by day; to die to all the corruptions of our old nature, and to live again, anew, in the charity of God. As St Paul told us in Sunday's Epistle lesson, without that charity, all else is useless. Without charity, prophecy, and knowledge, and even faith, are useless. Without charity, good works and self-sacrifice are ultimately useless. 'It profiteth one nothing,' says St Paul.

What then is this charity which must be the character and the substance of our Lenten journey? First of all, it is, of course, God's charity for us; that charity whereby he gave his only-begotten Son to be our justification. Secondly, it is the working of that charity in us, transforming our minds and hearts which is our sanctification. But just what is this charity – 'the very bond of peace and of all virtues,' as Sunday's Collect put it – Just what is this charity?

Fundamentally, it is steadfast and active good will. It's not sentiment, it's not emotion; it's not good works; although all those things may sometimes be associated with it. Fundamentally, it is steadfast and active good will: it is God's good will, manifest on Calvary; it is our good will, the gift of God's grace in us, when we steadfastly and actively will the eternal good of one another for God's sake. Charity is a habit of clarity and purity of motive in all we are and do; charity is our sanctification, as individuals and as a community.

That is what the spiritual journey of Lent is all about: it is to be a means of our sanctification, and growing up in charity, putting away the 'childish things' of old inclinations, desires, and predilections. The season of Lent is a time for putting aside our manifold distractions; a time for looking at what we are and what we do; a time to realize afresh that the charity of God

THE SOUL'S PILGRIMAGE

for us, and within us, and among us, is all that finally counts, and that without it, all else is just nonsense: 'sounding brass and tinkling cymbal.'

'Behold, we go up to Jerusalem,' to find our treasure there; and 'where your treasure is, there will your heart be also.'

Amen.

LENT I

*Then was Jesus led up of the Spirit into the wilderness
to be tempted of the devil.*

In the Gospel lesson for this first Sunday in Lent, we have St Matthew's account of the temptations of Jesus. This lesson is clearly intended to establish in our minds the meaning and the message of the Lenten season, and we should examine it with careful attention. And perhaps before we do that, it would be useful to think for a moment about the background and context of the story.

Jesus' fasting and temptations follow immediately upon his baptism. John the Baptist had come up out of the wilderness, preaching the baptism of repentance, preaching the advent of God's kingdom; and in the baptism of Jesus, John's prophetic mission was fulfilled. Here was the longed-for messiah, 'he that should come' – here was the Messiah, sealed by the descent of the Spirit, and the divine commendation, 'this is my beloved son'. Here, at long last, was the inauguration of God's new kingdom, long looked for by prophets and martyrs of Israel, and implicit in the longings and aspirations of the Gentile sages. All the hopes and expectations, all the desires of countless years, came to a focus in that man from Nazareth. But what, precisely, was the nature and meaning of his kingdom? That was yet to be made clear.

That is where today's Gospel story begins: 'Then was Jesus

THE SOUL'S PILGRIMAGE

led up of the Spirit into the wilderness to be tempted – to be tested – by the devil,' and it was there, in the wilderness – the place of barrenness, and peril, and privation; it was there that clarification came. It was there that the terms of the struggle for God's kingdom, the age-long conflict of good and evil, of light and darkness, became fully explicit; the devil, that is to say, was manifest. In the temptations of Jesus, the nature and forms of the conflict were made clear.

First, Jesus is tempted to turn stones into bread – to turn the divine power to serve immediate worldly ends; to satisfy the cravings of the senses. Not that the senses are in themselves evil; not that there is anything evil in being hungry and wanting to eat; the temptation lies rather in looking upon such satisfactions as the central and essential point of God's kingdom. For the kingdom of God does not consist in eating and drinking; it does not consist in miraculous devices for making the world more convenient. 'One does not live by bread alone, but by the whole Word of God.'

The second temptation is to test the divine power: 'If thou be the Son of God, cast thyself down …'. It is the temptation to measure the divine power, to control and manipulate the divine spirit, in one's own terms. But a god who is subject to human whim and human caprice is not the true and living God. God's kingdom is not and can never be a matter of using God. The miracles of his kingdom have quite another character and purpose. We may, indeed we should, raise to him our earnest intercession in time of need; but we must never presume to manipulate his power. 'Thou shalt not tempt the Lord thy God.'

The third temptation is the most fundamental, and indeed, it is the root of all the others. It is the ancient diabolical temptation of Adam in the Garden, to be as God. It is the temptation to

LENT I

set one's finite self in the place of God; to see oneself – one's own opinions and inclinations and experience – as the absolute measure of truth and goodness. That is really to worship the devil: 'All these things will I give thee, if thou wilt fall down and worship me.' It is, of course, an illusion, a futile pride and ambition, because it is untrue to the absolute reality of God, and the objective truth of his creation. 'Thou shalt worship the Lord thy God, and him only shalt thou serve.'

'Then the devil leaveth him.' The devil is unmasked. The illusions are revealed for what they are: the temptations to try to use God for worldly ends; the temptation to regard one's finite self as God. Once they are unmasked, they are, of course, absurd. There is nothing really so fundamentally absurd as the devil. But humankind has great capacity for wilful blindness and self-deception.

'And, behold, angels came and ministered unto him.' With the devil unmasked, with the illusions dispelled, Jesus is free in the charity of his vocation, and the angels – the pure and everlasting principles of the just order of God's universe – will serve him.

These temptations – these testings – of Jesus represent the essential forms of all temptation. They are our temptations, and the temptations of the Church. They are the illusions that we can use the divine Spirit for worldly ends, that we can make God subject to our whims, that we can be absolute, as God.

In this season of Lent, we are led up by the Spirit into the wilderness, to be tested; and the point is that we should be freed from our diabolical illusions. That is the point of our Gospel lesson for the next two Sundays. Just as God's ancient people were delivered from Egyptian bondage to attain the freedom of the promised land, only by way of forty years of struggle

THE SOUL'S PILGRIMAGE

through the wilderness, just so the forty-day pilgrimage of Lent engages us now in spiritual struggle, to liberate our souls, to liberate the Church, from the chains of captivity in an Egypt of worldly illusions.

The Church's lessons for this season sketch out for us, with an acute and unremitting logic, the stages of that struggle. Just try reading the Epistle and Gospel lessons for the Lenten Sundays as an ordered series, and I think you'll see what I mean: the casting out of all the demons which beguile us, not by Beelzebul, the chief of devils, but by the finger of God's Word; then the refurbishing of the swept and garnished house, not by more and still more subtle demons, but by the Word of God, wondrously multiplied here in the wilderness, by the nutriment of the heavenly Jerusalem, which is above, and is free. Then in Passiontide is set before us the principle and ground of our liberation and our nutriment, in the Passover of our saviour through death and resurrection – the Passover to the promised land of new life in the Spirit.

'Led up by the Spirit into the wilderness': we are led by the Spirit to discern the wilderness around us and within us – the wilderness of a confused and mixed-up world; the wilderness of a worldly Church; the wilderness of our own uncertain, muddled souls; the wilderness in which unknown perils and privations will confront us, and vicious serpents lurk to wound us. But that wilderness must not be evaded: it is, as Dante puts it, at the beginning of the *Inferno*, 'that rough and stubborn forest, in which I found great good'. It is only in the trials of the wilderness – 'in much patience, in afflictions, in necessities, in distresses', as St Paul says in today's Epistle – it is only in those trials that the saving virtues of faith and hope and love are forged – 'Like as silver,' says the psalmist, 'Which

LENT I

from the earth is tried and purified seven times in the fire.'

Only in and through the wilderness and all its struggles do we find the road that leads us to Jerusalem. Lent calls us to undertake afresh that road, in obedience and humility; to embrace our trials, and bless God for them; to take into our hands and into our hearts that heavenly manna which will sustain our pilgrimage. Our journey is the work of grace in us, and let us pray, with St Paul, 'that we receive not that grace in vain', for 'behold, now is the accepted time, now is the day of salvation.'

Amen.

LENT II

O woman, great is thy faith: be it unto thee even as thou wilt.

In our Gospel lessons for these Lenten Sundays, we hear a great deal about devils. Last Sunday, we heard about Jesus being 'led up by the spirit into the wilderness, to be tempted by the devil'. In today's Gospel, the Canaanite woman implores Jesus to save her daughter, who 'is vexed with a devil'; and in next Sunday's Gospel, Jesus is accused of casting out devils 'through Beelzebul, the prince of the devils'. The message of Lent seems much concerned with devils, and with what can and should be done about them.

But what, really, are we to make of such stories as these? Who, or what, are these devils?

In the Bible, and in the older history of religious literature and art, Christian and non-Christian, they seem to have a prominent place; but for many modern readers, I suspect, these old stories seem very strange. Talk about devils seems weird, and occult, and even superstitious. Devils seem to be nothing more than products of unhealthy imagination, characters in rather unpleasant fairy-tales; and sensible, modern people are not inclined to take them very seriously.

But this is really no matter of fairy-tale and superstition, and our Gospel lessons should remind us that it is a grave mistake to underestimate the reality and power of devils. No doubt our vocabulary in such matters has changed a good deal since

LENT II

ancient times, but the realities of spiritual life remain very much the same; and the devils are very much with us still, around us and within us. Basically, devils are wicked, unclean, perverse spiritual powers, perverse spiritual principles, and ideals, by which we are constantly tempted, and often governed.

To be 'vexed by a devil' means to have one's will, indeed one's whole personality, fixed and focused upon some spiritual perversion – some worldly lust, some idle curiosity, some vain ambition – to have one's will fixed upon some finite good, as though it were divine. It means to be devoted to some false god, devoted to some worldly idol of one sort or another. Their name indeed is 'Legion'.

It's not just a mistake – it's the willing of a fantasy, the willing of a lie. And he who wills a lie is possessed, and consumed, and incapacitated by that lie, mentally and physically. We do, of course, make mistakes and we are, of course troubled by all sorts of accidents and problems in the ordinary course of nature. To be possessed by a devil is something quite other than all that; to be possessed is to will a lie, to espouse and love a lie, as though it were the truth, and every one of us is vulnerable to such pretense in many more or less subtle forms.

In today's Gospel story, the Canaanite woman begs Jesus to deliver her daughter, who is 'grievously vexed by a devil'. In the Gospel stories, details are always significant; and in this story, it is particularly significant that the petitioner is a Canaanite. The Canaanites, as you will perhaps remember, were the old pagan population of Palestine, whom the Israelites tried to expel when they took possession of their promised land: and those Canaanites who remained, remained as despised outcaste. Thus the Canaanite woman is as far as possible from having any claim upon the 'children's bread', any natural right in

THE SOUL'S PILGRIMAGE

the nation of Israel, the commonwealth of God. But she comes, nevertheless, in humility and trust: 'The little dogs' she says, those who have no rights, 'eat of the crumbs which fall from their master's table.' And the grace of God, unmerited by any natural claims, is not withheld: 'O woman, great is thy faith; be it unto thee as thou wilt.' This Canaanite woman is the symbol of all of us, who have no natural claims upon God's favour. Jesus' gift to her stands for the free, unmerited grace of God.

'O woman, great is thy faith.' It is only in relation to faith that his grace of healing comes. That is to say, it is only in the recognition of the true and living God that we are delivered from the false gods, those fantasies which are our devils. We can perhaps cast out one devil in favour of another, but that is no deliverance. As next Sunday's Gospel explains, 'When the unclean spirit is gone out of a man, he walketh through dry places, seeking rest; and finding none, he saith, "I will return unto my house whence I came out"; and when he cometh, he findeth it swept and garnished; then goeth he and taketh to him seven other spirits more wicked than himself, and they enter in and dwell there; and the last state of that man is worse than the first.' It is only faith, only the recognition of the true and living God, which brings deliverance. Simply to cast out one false god is simply to invite another in.

Disillusionment is not enough. The empty soul is no solution — it only invites the bitter devils of cynicism to come and dwell therein. Deliverance comes only as our souls are filled, our minds renewed, with God — nourished and nurtured by his living Word.

Lent is a season of renewal and reformation: 'Be not conformed to this present age, but be ye transformed by the renewing of your mind.' It is a time for the casting out of devils,

LENT II

the unmasking of the perversions of our spirits, a time for the nurturing of our souls by the Word of God revealed in Christ our Lord. It is a time of death and resurrection.

We come as the Canaanite woman came – not with any particular merit, not with any natural claim upon the grace of God. But we come, nevertheless, with faith and hope in the abundant charity of that grace. Perhaps a crumb is all we seek; but he calls us to be his table guests, to share the rich banquet of his Word.

Amen.

LENT III

When a strong man armed keepeth his palace,
his goods are in peace; but when a stronger than
he shall come upon him and overcome him,
he taketh away from him all his armour wherein
he trusted, and divideth his spoils.

A great military leader, who was also President of the United States, once told reporters that his favourite biblical text was this: 'When a strong man armed keepeth his house, his goods are in peace.' The text seemed to lend divine authority to the doctrine of military preparedness. But quoting verses of scripture out of context can be hazardous. The President had apparently not noticed that the 'strong man armed' in this verse refers to the devil; and the verse goes on to say that 'when a stronger than he' – that is, Christ – 'shall come upon him and overcome him, he taketh away from him all his armour wherein he trusted, and divideth his spoils'. It is not a statement about the value of military power at all, but about weakness of demonic powers in comparison with the Word of God to overcome them and cast them out.

No doubt it is a somewhat obscure and difficult text: what, really, are these demonic powers, and how are they cast out? Scripture has a great deal to say about devils, and on the first three Sundays in Lent, in particular, we hear a lot about them. Jesus was first tempted by the devil in the wilderness; the

LENT III

Canaanite woman's daughter was grievously vexed with a devil, and in today's Gospel lesson, 'Jesus was casting out a devil, and it was dumb.'

Devils seem to have been very much a part of the scenery. The bystanders in today's story were in no doubt about the reality of these devils, but only about how Jesus managed to cast them out. Some of them suspected that he must have some sort of pact with the chief devil, Beelzebul (or Lucifer), and demanded proof of his credentials – 'a sign from heaven'.

Our vocabulary in such matters has changed a good deal since ancient times. We have little to say about devils, and these old stories from the Bible sound very peculiar: they seem to smack of the weird, or occult, or superstitious. 'Beelzebul' and his crew seem like characters out of rather unpleasant fairy-tales.

But this is no matter of fairy-tale, and certainly is not a matter of superstition. Although our vocabulary has changed, the experience of devils is still very much with us. To be possessed by a devil means to have one's will fixed upon some finite person or thing as though it were absolute – as though it were God. Devils are not simply evil: Lucifer was, after all, the highest and best of creatures – the angel of light: his fall consisted in his claim to be 'as God', his fixation upon himself as absolute. It's not just a mistake, it's the willing of fantasy, a willing of a lie. And he who wills a lie is possessed and consumed and incapacitated by that lie, mentally and physically. That's what it means, I think, to be possessed by a devil, and I suppose that's not an uncommon predicament in any age, although our language for describing it may change.

And how are these devils cast out? Not by Beelzebul, the prince of the devils – not by the ultimate lie. Satan's kingdom

THE SOUL'S PILGRIMAGE

is a kingdom of lies, 'and if Satan be divided against himself, how shall his kingdom stand?' Devils are cast out only by the authority of truth, revealing, unmasking the lie: puncturing the pretence, reproving the unfruitful works of darkness by the light of truth.

'All these things that are reproved are made manifest by the light,' says St Paul, 'for whatsoever doth make manifest is light.'

This casting out is a kind of disillusionment: the casting away of fantasies and illusions, seeing through the lie. But disillusionment – about oneself and other people and the good things of creation – is not enough. 'When the unclean spirit is gone out of a man, he walketh through dry places seeking rest, and finding none, he saith, "I will return to my house whence I came out"; and when he cometh he findeth it swept and garnished; then goeth he and taketh to him seven other spirits more wicked than himself, and they enter in and dwell there; and the last state of the man is worse than the first.'

In our age of enlightened secularism, there are many disillusioned souls, for whom nothing is absolute; souls who see that you can't trust anybody absolutely; souls who see that the goods of this world are limited and transitory. But this disillusionment adds up to a kind of cynicism, a spiritual emptiness: the house is 'swept and garnished'. But the sense of the absolute, the thirst for the absolute will not be denied, and the devils return, more viciously than ever, and in very bizarre forms. I think that explains the significance of certain demonic religious cults just now: they come to the disillusioned, the spiritually empty.

The Word of God is certainly a disillusioning word: it penetrates and criticizes and unmasks our fantasies and our lies; it puts its finger on our devils. Sometimes, through very tough

LENT III

experiences, it shatters our illusions. But it does not leave us empty – it reveals to us the Absolute, which is not ourselves, nor any created thing. And in that disillusioning and revealing Word must be our confidence. 'If I by the finger of God cast out devils, no doubt the kingdom of God hath come upon you.'

Certainly, the devil is 'a strong man armed'; but 'a stronger than he has come.'

> And were this world all devils o'er,
> And watching to devour us,
> We lay it not to heart so sore;
> Not they can overpower us.
> And let the prince of ill
> Look grim as e'er he will,
> He harms us not a whit;
> For why? – his doom is writ;
> A word shall quickly slay him.

Amen.

LENT IV

*Stand fast therefore in the liberty wherewith
Christ hath made us free.*

This mid-Lent Sunday has a variety of names: it is sometimes called '*Laetare* Sunday'; '*Laetare*' being the first word of the ancient Latin introit: 'Rejoice ye with Jerusalem, and be glad with her, all ye that love her.' And the propers for today do indeed sound a note of rejoicing in the midst of the rather sombre sobriety of Lent. Another very ancient name is '*Dominica Refectionis*' – 'Refreshment Sunday'; no doubt an allusion to the Gospel story of the feeding of the five thousand in the wilderness. Yet another name is 'Mothering Sunday', having reference to St Paul's identification of the free and heavenly Jerusalem as 'the mother of us all'; and in the British Isles, especially, this Sunday has been traditionally observed as Mother's Day, when children would come home to visit their mothers, and their mother Church, with gifts of flowers and seed cakes.

It is then a day of rejoicing and refreshment – a break in the austerity and watchfulness of Lent. And in some churches today, rose-coloured vestments are worn instead of the solemn purple of Lent, marking this difference. The Collect, which is a translation of the ancient Latin collect, marks the idea with the prayer that we may be relieved by the comfort of God's grace. That we may be relieved: '*ut respirimus*' the Latin says; that we may breathe again – catch our breath – really it's a sigh of relief.

LENT IV

And the Epistle carries on this idea, dwelling on the glad freedom of the Gospel covenant of love, as distinguished from the bondage of the law, riveted by fear. This passage from Galatians is a remarkable piece of symbolic interpretation of the Old Testament. 'Tell me,' says St Paul, 'Ye that desire to be under the law, do ye not hear the law? For it is written that Abraham had two sons, the one by a bond-maid, the other by a free-woman, But he that was born of the bond-woman was born after the flesh; but he of the free-woman was by promise. Which things are an allegory ...'

Perhaps you remember the story in Genesis. Sarah, Abraham's wife, was barren, and he had a son, Ishmael, by Hagar, a bond-maid, who was his concubine. Then, when Abraham and Sarah were both very old, they were miraculously given a child of their own, Isaac, who was then Abraham's legitimate heir.

'Which things are an allegory,' says St Paul. Not explaining away the simple historical sense but using a symbolical interpretation to bring out the general principles it exemplifies, he goes on to explain, that Hagar and Sarah stand for the two covenants, the old and the new. Hagar, the bond-maid, represents the law. She stands for Mount Sinai, the mountain of the commandments. She stands for the earthly Jerusalem, the city of worldly hopes, 'Jerusalem which now is, and is in bondage with her children' – in bondage to the law, in the spirit of fear. Sarah, the free-woman, stands for the covenant of promise, in the free spirit of charity: she stands for heavenly city, which is free, and is our true mother.

He who clings to the law is, like Ishmael, a child of nature and of bondage, a citizen of the earthly city which now is; having no inheritance in God's kingdom. We are called to be, like Isaac was, children of the promise, the spirit, citizens and legitimate heirs of the Jerusalem which is above.

'For ye have not received the spirit of bondage again to fear … For ye are sons and if sons, then heirs; heirs of God, and joint-heirs with Christ.'

'What saith the scripture? Cast out the bond-woman and her son; for the son of the bond-woman shall not be heir with the son of the free-woman.' That is to say, following St Paul's argument, our old nature, our worldliness, which is really bondage, is to be cast off: the inheritance of the saints demands our freedom from that bondage; that we grasp the promises of God, that we grasp in faith and hope our true end which is not any external law; our true end, which is nothing less than the knowledge and love of God himself: 'Heirs of God, and joint-heirs with Christ.' 'So then, brethren, we are not children of the bond-woman, but of the free. Stand fast, therefore, in the liberty wherewith Christ hath made us free.'

I think that the worldliness of Hagar and Ishmael is very much our problem. 'That which is born of the flesh is flesh,' and we are very much attached to that Jerusalem which now is, that earthly city with all its worldly hopes: so much attached, perhaps, that the heavenly city seems little more than the vaguely pleasant never-never land of fairy tales. Even in our churches, world-improvement is often urged upon us as though it were the end of our vocation as Christians – as though worldly comfort and convenience for all were the ultimate objectives of Christian charity. Sometimes this view of things is dignified by the name of 'Incarnational Christianity'.

Now world improvement is certainly a good thing, and we have surely made great strides in that direction: even if some of our intended improvements turn out to be somewhat ambiguous.

LENT IV

And certainly Christian charity requires that we act as seriously as possible to relieve suffering and provide comfort where we can. But to suppose that the perfecting of the world in that sense is the end for human souls is a sad and dangerous delusion.

Incomparably more realistic is the twelfth-century poet, Bernard of Cluny, when he says:

> Brief life is here our portion,
> Brief sorrow, short-lived care;
> The life that knows no ending,
> The tearless life, is there.

'That which is born of the flesh is flesh' yes, but, 'that which is born of the Spirit is spirit'. And spirit will have nothing less than God's eternity, the heavenly Jerusalem. This world is the wilderness of our trial – the realm of our struggles with our own particular devils, and their name seems to be Legion. With Hagar and Ishmael, we wander disconsolate. 'How can anyone satisfy these men with bread here in the wilderness?'

But Refreshment Sunday bids us look up. In the wilderness of our pilgrimage there is miraculously multiplied for us the heavenly bread of God's grace. Angels bear us up, and there is set before our eyes the vision of that city which is above and is free, Jerusalem, our mother; and in that vision and nourished by that bread, we can stand fast in the liberty with which Christ has made us free. And Bernard of Cluny finishes his poem:

> The morning shall awaken,
> The shadows shall decay,
> And each true-hearted servant
> Shall shine as doth the day.

THE SOUL'S PILGRIMAGE

Then all the halls of Sion
For ay shall be complete,
And in the Land of Beauty
All things of beauty meet.

Amen.

PASSION SUNDAY
FIRST SERMON

*Whosoever will be great among you,
let him be your minister.*

Zebedee's wife seems to have been surprisingly optimistic about the political prospects of Jesus. She was proud of her two sons James and John, who were among the closest followers of Jesus, and she asked Jesus to do something special for them when he came to power. Her ambition seems natural enough, and her straightforward honesty is really almost touching: she wanted the best for her boys. 'She saith unto him, "Grant that these my two sons may sit, the one on thy right hand, and the other on thy left in thy kingdom".'

'But Jesus answered and said, 'Ye know not what ye ask. Are ye able to drink of the cup that I shall drink of, and to be baptized with the baptism that I am baptized with?' The coming of his kingdom would not be quite the sort of thing the ambitious mother had in mind. Jesus knew that it would involve the bitter cup of his Passion, and the baptism of his own blood shed on Calvary. But the impetuous sons, James and John, whom he had nicknamed 'Boanerges' – 'Sons of thunder' – were quick to assure him that they could endure any hardships which might be in store. 'We are able,' they say.

Well, yes, certainly they would share in the Passion of

THE SOUL'S PILGRIMAGE

Jesus, but still their mother's request was impossible: 'To sit on my right hand, and on my left, is not mine to give, but it shall be given to them for whom it is prepared of my Father.' That is to say, the rewards of God's kingdom are not like political patronage, distributed to faithful party workers. Remember the Gospel lesson for Septuagesima Sunday: those who came to the vineyard at the eleventh hour received the same as those who had borne the burden and heat of the day. The rewards of God's kingdom are not according to worldly merit, but only according to the free grace and mercy of God. We do not earn a place in heaven. God owes us nothing.

James and John and their mother must have been rather disappointed and puzzled by Jesus' answer; and to top it all off, the other disciples were angry about this request for special preferment. 'The ten were moved with indignation against the two brethren.' But the other disciples were really no wiser in their indignation than James and John had been in their request. And so Jesus gathered them all around him, and used the occasion to teach them all an important lesson; and his explanation is really the essential message of Passiontide.

'Ye know that the princes of the Gentiles exercise dominion over them, and they that are great exercise authority upon them.' That is to say, there are certain worldly ways of doing things and looking at things which James and John and the other ten have in common. They are like the 'princes of the Gentiles,' for whom greatness is a matter of worldly power and domination. But in the kingdom of God, says Jesus, that is not the way things are: 'It shall not be so among you: but whosoever will be great among you, let him be your minister; and whosoever will be chief among you, let him be your servant.'

PASSION SUNDAY FIRST SERMON

That is to say, the kingdom of God requires a reversal of perspective, a reversal of attitude. I said that the ambition of Zebedee's wife seemed natural, and I think that it is indeed natural, in worldly terms. The point is that the kingdom of God requires an inversion, an overturning, of our 'natural' worldliness: 'whosoever will be great among you, let him be your minister, whosoever will be chief among you, let him be your servant.'

This is the essential lesson of Passiontide. We celebrate at once a kingship and a crucifixion. They are not separate: the ignominious cross is the throne of glory. Consider the words of Fortunatus' marvellous hymn:

> Fulfilled is all his words foretold:
> Then spread the banners, and unfold
> Love's crowning power, that all may see
> He reigns and triumphs from the Tree.

'He reigns and triumphs from the Tree.' It's a strange kingship, surely, and one which the world finds incomprehensible. Pilate didn't know what to make of it: 'Art thou a king, then?' he asked. 'The princes of the Gentiles exercise dominion' – what kind of dominion is this? Here is no dominion but the monarchy of love, which endures when all worldly dominions are long gone in dust and ashes.

Lent leads into Passiontide, and it is in the Passion of Jesus that all the lessons of Lent are summed up. The whole point of Lenten discipline is that the demons of worldliness, the demons of false and empty ambitions and expectations should be cast out of us: 'It shall not be so among you' – and that we should be filled with the living bread which comes from heaven, the Word

THE SOUL'S PILGRIMAGE

of God himself, who comes, 'not to be ministered unto, but to minister, and to give his life as a ransom for many'.

We do not learn such lessons easily. 'By the finger of God'; our demons are cast out; but sometimes there's a great struggle: some kinds of demons, as Jesus says, are cast out only with much prayer and fasting. The attitude of Zebedee's wife seems all too natural, and that old nature seems very strong. 'When a strong man armed keepeth his palace, his goods are in peace; but when a stronger than he shall come upon him, he taketh from him all his armour wherein he trusted, and divideth the spoils.' The 'princes of the Gentiles' seem strong in their dominion, but surely the Word of God unmasks their pretensions as nothing but dust and ashes in the end.

'Whosoever will be great among you,' therefore, 'let him be your minister; and whosoever will be chief among you, let him be your servant: even as the Son of Man came not to be ministered unto, but to minister, and to give his life a ransom for many.'

Amen.

PASSION SUNDAY SECOND SERMON

The princes of the Gentiles exercise dominion over them ... but it shall not be so among you.

Our lectionary – that is, the series of Epistle and Gospel lessons appointed for Sundays and major festivals throughout the year – has remained substantially unchanged for well over a thousand years. Even through the tumults of the Reformation, the lectionary, taken over from medieval service books, remained largely intact, with only here and there a slight addition or subtraction of a few verses. That stable pattern of public readings, year by year, century by century, first in Latin, then in various vernaculars, has, of course, been immensely important for the shaping of the mind of Western Christendom; and it's a factor of which we should always be conscious when we try to understand the history of literature, or music, or the other arts, as well as the history of theology and popular piety.

Because the tradition is so venerable, and because alterations to it have been so slight, changes in it should attract our thoughtful attention. One such change, quite recent, introduced in our 1962 Canadian revision of the *Book of Common Prayer*, is the Gospel lesson for Passion Sunday (which we've just now read). The old lesson was the story of Jesus' final conflict with the Jewish authorities before the events of Holy Week.

THE SOUL'S PILGRIMAGE

Now, instead, we have the story of Zebedee's wife, and her sons, James and John. It's a change which somewhat disrupts the logical pattern of the lectionary; but it's also a change which introduces a striking and important emphasis in the Church's proclamation of Christ's Passion.

When I say that this change somewhat disrupts the logical pattern of the lectionary, I mean that, in general, the Gospel lessons for Lent and Passiontide set before our minds and hearts what Christ has done and suffered for us; while the Epistle lessons spell out the practical implications of that for our own lives, to show us how the sacrifice of Christ must, as today's Epistle, for instance, puts it, 'purify our conscience from dead works to serve the living God'.

Christ's sacrifice is not only something done *for* us, once for all; it is that, certainly; but it is also something which is done *in* us, in our minds and hearts, day by day. Our faithful and thankful acceptance of Christ's work for us must also change us, must transform our minds and hearts, must sanctify our lives.

It is that side of the matter – our sanctification – that our Gospel lesson insists upon. The way of Christ's Passion demands in us an inner change of direction, a reversal of perspective, a different aspiration, a conversion. In today's story, the standpoint of the natural man is perfectly represented by James and John, by their mother, and by the whole band of disciples. Their aspirations are surely perfectly natural human ambitions. But Jesus contradicts those aspirations, and points a different way. 'You know,' he says, 'that the princes of the Gentiles exercise dominion over them.' That is to say, there are certain worldly ways of doing things, certain worldly desires and ambitions: for the Gentiles, greatness is a matter of power and dominion, sitting on the right hand of majesty, having one's own way. But

PASSION SUNDAY SECOND SERMON

in the kingdom of God, says Jesus, that's not the way things are: 'It shall not be so among you.' Your greatness, your dignity, your nobility, is the humble obedience of the servant. And there – you see – is the essential meaning of Passiontide for our own inner lives, our conversion.

Lent leads into Passiontide, and it is in the Passion of Jesus that all the lessons of Lent are summed up: the demons in the wilderness, the demons of worldliness, the demons of false and empty ambitions and aspirations, all the destructive and self-destructive demons of self-seeking must be cast out from us, 'by the finger of God'. 'It shall not be so among you.' Our souls must be filled, instead, with the living bread from heaven, miraculously multiplied for us here in the wilderness: the Word of God himself, the word of obedient and sacrificial love, which is both death and resurrection; death, day by day, to our old and worldly selves, but a new birth in us, day by day, of a life which is eternal.

In our liturgy, we celebrate Christ's Passion, the sacrifice of Calvary, represented here in bread and wine, the signs of body broken and blood outpoured. We celebrate the presence of his sacrifice, as something done for us once for all, a full, perfect and sufficient sacrifice, something which we gaze upon with adoration and with thankful hearts; but that same sacrifice, we know, must also be something done in us; it must be our food and drink, it must have its way in the transformation of our minds and hearts. 'Let this mind be in you, which was also in Christ Jesus….'

Amen.

PALM SUNDAY

Let this mind be in you, which was also in Christ Jesus.

On Palm Sunday, we celebrate the kingship of our Lord and Saviour, Jesus Christ. We celebrate the dramatic moment of his triumph, as he enters Jerusalem, the holy city, and all the children cry, 'Hosanna to the son of David! Blessed is he that cometh in the name of the Lord!' He comes as the promised son of David, the messianic king 'meek and riding upon an ass'. There is no mistaking the symbolism of the occasion: the ecstatic multitudes acclaim their king and cast down garments and palm branches in the way to make a royal path for him. The Pharisees demand that he dismiss this noisy crowd, but Jesus simply answers, 'I tell you, if these should hold their peace, the very stones would cry out.'

He comes as messianic king to David's royal city, and the multitudes acclaim his coming: 'Hosanna to the Son of David.' It seems a moment of great triumph, as he enters the holy city and goes on to cleanse the temple at the city's heart. It seems a moment of great triumph; but how quickly is that moment overshadowed by the terrible events which follow. Jerusalem cannot accept this king. It cannot understand his kingship; it will deny him, and he will be crucified outside its gates. 'O Jerusalem, Jerusalem, thou that killest the prophets, behold, thy house shall be left unto thee desolate.'

PALM SUNDAY

The whole business seems full of tragic contradiction. As Dean Crossman puts it in his lovely hymn:

> Sometimes they strew his way,
> And his sweet praises sing;
> Resounding all the day
> Hosannas to their king,
> Then 'Crucify'
> Is all their breath.
> And for his death
> They thirst and cry.

The whole affair seems contradictory; and today's liturgy mirrors precisely that contradiction. We sing the glorious and triumphal ninth-century hymn, 'All Glory, Laud and Honor to Thee Redeemer King'. We bless and distribute the branches of palm, the symbols of his kingship; and then we read the Passion according to St Matthew, that cruel and violent story of the condemnation of the just and innocent.

It seems such a tragic and painful contradiction. But in that very contradiction, there is a simple and powerful, and all-important message, which sums up all the lessons of this Lenten season. The point is this: the kingship of Jesus, true kingship, liberty, and dignity, do not consist in worldly pomp and power, in worldly glory and ambition, nor in worldly grace and beauty: 'Lo, we have seen him without form or comeliness.' Stripped of all these things, 'spitefully entreated and spitted on,' then, precisely then, he manifests true kingship. The ancient hymn for Passiontide by Fortunatus makes the point with great poetic genius.

THE SOUL'S PILGRIMAGE

Fulfilled is all his words foretold
Then spread the banners, and unfold
Love's crowning power, that all may see
He reigns and triumphs from the Tree.

'Are you a king, then?' asks Pilate. Yes, he is indeed a king. 'Thou sayst it.' But kingship is not what Pilate thinks it is; not what the world thinks it is. Yes, he is the king; 'But now is my kingdom not from hence: if it were, then would my servants fight … but now is my kingdom not from hence.'

In the events of Passiontide, there is a dramatic transformation of the very idea of kingship. What is really going on here is a complete overturning of conventional worldly attitudes and understandings about what constitutes true kingship, true freedom, and true dignity. The lesson here has been present in one form or another in all the scripture lessons of the Lenten season, beginning with the story of Jesus' rejection of his own temptations. It was perhaps especially explicit in last Sunday's Gospel. Remember how the mother of Zebedee's children, the mother of James and John, came to Jesus asking him a favour: 'Grant that my two sons may sit, one on your right hand and the other on your left in your kingdom.' 'You do not know what you ask,' said Jesus. The assumptions behind the request were all wrong. Surely, they are the natural and nearly inevitable assumptions of every one of us, and how surely are they conformed to the present age. But those assumptions are all wrong, says Jesus. 'The princes of the gentiles lord it over them … but it shall not be so among you.' God's kingdom and the glory of its kingship are altogether different. Its kingship is the kingship of a servant, its liberty is the liberty of free obedience, its virtue is humility.

PALM SUNDAY

'Let this mind be in you, which was also in Christ Jesus.' Those words of St Paul sum it up magnificently. 'Let this mind be in you, which was also in Christ Jesus … who took upon himself the form of a servant, and became obedient even unto death.' In his word, and in his Passion, Jesus proclaims that the pomps and glories of the world are vain and that our trust in them is ruinous. True kingship requires the rejection of all that and the casting out of all those worldly demons which possess our soul. 'My kingdom,' says Jesus, 'is not from hence.'

The signs of his royal glory are the signs of his humility, of his suffering, of his Passion. The signs of his glory are the signs of body broken, and blood outpoured. 'He reigns and triumphs from the Tree.' That is the glory we celebrate on Palm Sunday and that is the glory we show forth day by day in the Church's liturgy as we break the bread and drink the cup. And that is the glory which must adorn our lives, for we are called to be a kingly priesthood. The lesson is simple and all-important. O, that we could begin to grasp it in the living of our lives.

'Let this mind be in you, which was also in Christ Jesus.' That is the renewal of our minds, to which the Gospel calls us that we 'should follow the example of his great humility', and thus be made partaker of his life.

Amen.

TUESDAY IN HOLY WEEK

*Therefore have I set my face like a flint,
and I know that I shall not be ashamed.*

The feature which chiefly characterizes the Church's liturgy in Holy Week is the solemn reading of the Passion of our Lord and saviour Jesus Christ. We begin on Palm Sunday, reading the Passion according to St Matthew; on Monday and Tuesday, the Passion according to St Mark; on Wednesday and Thursday, the Passion according to St Luke, and on Friday – Good Friday – we finish with the Passion according to St John.

It is as though we would not miss one minutest detail of these ancient reports of the torture, condemnation, and crucifixion of Christ our Lord.

In many ways these lessons make painful and bitter reading: it is all so obviously, so pitifully unjust.

> Why, what hath my Lord done?
> What makes this rage and spite?
> He made the lame to run,
> He gave the blind their sight.
> Sweet injuries!

TUESDAY IN HOLY WEEK

> Yet they at these
> Themselves displease,
> And 'gainst him rise ...

It seems a bitter and tragic story of the condemnation and destruction of the just and innocent, and surely, as we look upon it, it moves the heart to pity and remorse. We can blame it all, of course, on ancient Jews and Romans, and even more specifically, on Judas, but somehow that will not do – we sense ourselves involved in that betrayal with Peter in his denial of the Christ, we think thereon and weep.

But that is not altogether the point of the reading of the Passion. It is clear that for the Gospel writers, and for Christian faith it is not just some tragic accident that could have been avoided, for which we should be sorry, but rather, all that happens there lies within the Providence of God, and all of it is freely willed by Christ our saviour:

> I came to do thy will, O my God – yea, I am content to do it, thy law is within my heart.

He set his face steadfastly, he set his face 'like a flint' – to go up to Jerusalem. And in the garden of Gethsemane, he prayed, 'O Father, if it be possible, let this cup pass from me: nevertheless, not as I will, but as Thou wilt.'

The causes and the meaning of the Passion lie deeper than the temporary perversity of the Roman and Jewish authorities of that particular time in Palestine, and deeper than the perfidy or the cowardice of Judas or of Pilate. The causes of the Passion lie deeper, and we must try to grasp their meaning more broadly, in terms of the whole providential

THE SOUL'S PILGRIMAGE

plan of the creation and redemption of humankind.

Simply put, the cause of our Lord's Passion is the free and willing disobedience of humankind, a disobedience which runs through the whole course of human history, not just first-century Palestine. The story of Adam and Eve, at the beginning of the book of Genesis is a story of our first parents: but it is much more than that – it is a story of a disobedience which runs through every age and every page of human history – a story of bloodshed and disaster of hopelessness and tragedy. It is the story of Abel slain at his brother's hand. It is the story of Cain, wanderer upon the earth with the mark of guilt upon his brow. It is the story of a thousand massacres: it is the story of our ruthless exploitation of nature and fellow humans. It is a story echoed every day in every newspaper and every news report.

The symbol of all this is that tree in Eden's garden, the tree whereof God said we might not eat; yet we were persuaded, that it was good, and would make us Gods unto ourselves.

And so we ate – so we have eaten – and so we do eat. 'Who was the guilty? Who brought this upon thee? Alas, my treason, Jesu, hath undone Thee.'

Some of you must know that lovely legend, echoed in our Passiontide hymn, according to which the ancient tree of disobedience furnished the wood to make the cross of Calvary. That is purely legendary, of course; but its symbolism which connects those trees is profoundly true. For against that tree of ancient and ever new disobedience, stands the tree of Calvary.

Against all our disobedience, stands the obedience of Christ: 'I come to do Thy will, O my God – yea, I am content to do it, thy law is within my heart.'

TUESDAY IN HOLY WEEK

He set his face steadfastly, he set his face 'like a flint', to go up to Jerusalem. And in the new garden of obedience, he prayed, 'Thy will be done.' In obedience he was lifted up, upon the tree of the cross; against that ancient tree of disobedience, the tree of false pride and independence, he set the tree of his own final and complete obedience. And the leaves of this tree are for the healing of the nations.

And thus, the signs of his Passion become the signs of our redemption – 'Thorns and cross and nails and lance – These our rich inheritance.' The crown of thorns is the crown of glory, and the cross of suffering is decked in royal purple:

> O Tree of Grace, the conquering sign
> Which dost in royal purple shine,
> Gone is thy shame, for lo, each bough
> Proclaims the prince of glory now.

The Passion of our Lord and saviour Jesus Christ is finished. It is something accomplished centuries ago in that one act, our enmity with God is slain, our alienation is overcome. For Christ's sake, those who would be his are counted sons of God by grace – no longer enemies. It is a sacrifice once for all. And yet it would be wrong to think of it as simply something past. For here tonight, at the altar of this Church, we celebrate the presence of his Passion. As often as ye eat this bread and drink this cup, ye do show the Lord's death, until he come. We hold up, we show forth Christ's sacrifice, and plead that all sufficient offering.

We celebrate the presence of Calvary, under the signs of Body broken, and Blood outpoured. We celebrate the presence of the sacrifice of Christ – the sacrifice of his obedience, and we are to become what we celebrate. That is the message of our liturgy. That is the principle of obedient life in the midst of the chaos of a disobedient world; our worship is to be the sign and the effectual means of our obedience.

And thus, we read the Passion of our Lord and saviour and pray that we may have the grace of his obedience in our hearts and in our lives, 'that all mankind should follow the example of his patience, and also be made partakers of his resurrection'.

Amen.

MAUNDY THURSDAY
FIRST SERMON

Henceforth I call you not servants;
for the servant knoweth not what his lord doeth:
but I have called you friends; for all things
that I have heard of my Father,
I have made known unto you.

Jesus calls his disciples friends; and now he goes on to seal that friendship with friendship's highest token: 'For greater love hath no one than this, that a man lay down his life for his friends.' He gives himself tonight, in the sacrament; tomorrow on the cross. We are his friends, and not just his servants, because we know what our master is doing. Ours is the free and responsible relation of friends, because we understand his work, and share in it with a will which is our own and not another's. We understand, because all things that he has heard of his Father, he made known unto us.

But can we really understand all this? Surely the events of this Holy Week seem quite beyond the understanding and sympathy of friends. When the sun is darkened, and the veil of the Temple is rent in twain, when the earth quakes, and the rocks are rent, and hell itself is shaken, are we really his friends? No sympathy, no grief, no human compassion seems to fit the case. Much better the centurion's terrible fear: 'Truly this was the Son of God.'

This seems to be God's business rather than ours. As Homer's Alkinous says of the horrors of the Trojan war: 'That was all the work of gods, weaving ruin there, so it should make a song for men to come.' It seems to be God's business, far beyond us; perhaps a matter of horror and awe, if we catch a glimpse of its terrors, but hardly a matter of friendship. Friendship, surely, implies mutual understanding, mutual active benevolence, mutually recognized; and that involves an equality, or at least some proper proportion, between the parties.

What proportion can there possibly be between us and the dying Son of God? How can we be friends?

As Aristotle remarks:

> When there is a great interval in respect of virtue or vice or wealth, or anything else, between the parties, they are no longer friends, and do not even expect to be so. And this is most manifest in the case of the gods, for they surpass us decisively in all good things . . . when one party is removed to a great distance, as God is, the possibility of friendship ceases.

In general, Aristotle is right, as he usually is, especially in points of theology. But Aristotle could not know the unthinkable mercy of God in the Incarnation and Passion of Christ, whereby the distance of humanity from God is overcome and we are called friends. In the atoning sacrifice of Christ, God manifests the ultimate benevolence towards us: 'Greater love hath no man than this.' He manifests and makes known that benevolence and sets it in our hearts; and

MAUNDY THURSDAY FIRST SERMON

that is the principle and ground of our friendship with him. We are friends of God because his grace makes us so. He makes us God-like, and grants us the equality of friends, the proportional equality of sons. 'Behold what manner of love the Father hath bestowed upon us, that we should be called the sons of God.'

That is the friendship which Christians call 'charity', the very bond of peace and of all virtues, the friendship which binds us to God, and unites us to one another in the new commandment of love, 'Fellow-citizens with the saints, and of the household of God.' And as friends, we must do as friends do: we delight in God's presence; we rejoice in our converse with him, and find comfort in his consolations. As friends we care for all that is his. As friends, we seek to do his will, as free men, not as slaves. 'For we are in love,' says St Thomas, 'and it is from love we act, not from servile fear.'

Today is the day of the 'Maundy', the '*mandatum*', the new commandment of love; it is the day of friendship, and the traditional ceremonies of the day – the washing of feet, the blessing of oils for the sick, and so on – all reinforce that thought. Above all, it is the day of the banquet, the celebrations of friends, in which our friend gives himself, that we may dwell in him, and he in us. It is the moment of friends rejoicing together before the pain of tomorrow.

Soon we shall remove the trappings of the feast, and leave the altar bare and cold; for tonight is the night of betrayal, and tomorrow is the day of despair. But he has called us his friends, and we must watch with him, and 'not fear, though the earth be moved, and the mountains shake'. We must watch and pray that the bond of charity may hold us firm – his friends, and friends of one another. The fruit of the vine is crushed in the press, but we shall drink the wine new with him in the joy of his risen kingdom.

Amen.

MAUNDY THURSDAY
SECOND SERMON

The charity of Christ compels us.

Maundy Thursday is traditionally a day of many special ceremonies, all of them still to some extent observed in various parts of Christendom. There is, for instance, the ancient ceremony of the washing of the feet, in emulation of Christ's washing of his disciples' feet – an emblem of the charity we owe to one another. There is the ceremony of the Royal Maundy, the symbolic almsgiving of the Royal family. There is the bishop's blessing of the oils, for the anointing of the sick; and so on. All those ceremonies serve to emphasize that theme of the day; for this is Maundy Thursday, *Dies mandati* – the day of Christ's new commandment, that we love one another, as he has loved us. Today is the festival of charity.

The climax and focal point of all the Maundy ceremonies is, and has always been, since ancient times, the solemn and festive liturgy of the Lord's Supper. And that is so, not only by way of an historical commemoration of the institution of this blessed sacrament 'on the night in which he was betrayed'; it has also to do with the essential nature of the Eucharist as the sacrament of charity – expressive of the charity of Christ, and creative of his charity in us and amongst us. Thus, traditional theology, distinguishing between *res* and *sacramentum* – between the inner reality and the effect (*res*) and the sacramental sign – declares that the *res* of this sacrament is the grace of charity: that charity whereby Christ dwells in us and we in him.

We may speak of 'love', but that is not precise enough; 'charity' means something more precise. At the institution of this sacrament, our saviour says to the disciples that he will not call them servants; he will call them friends. Charity, explains St Thomas, means not just the love of God, but a certain friendship with him, which adds to love a mutuality of loving, and mutual communication. As it is said in the First Epistle of St John: 'He who dwells in charity dwells in God, and God in him.' And because it belongs especially to friendship that one dwell with one's friends, Christ does not leave us bereft of his presence, but through his body and his blood, he joins us to him in this sacrament; as he says in St John's Gospel, 'He who eats my flesh and drinks my blood, dwells in me and I in him.' Whence, says St Thomas, this sacrament is the highest sign of charity. Therefore, this liturgy is not just another Maundy ceremony, but the essential one, Christ's own Royal Maundy, the very charter and basis of our life of charity with him and one another, which all the other ceremonies symbolically suggest.

This evening's liturgy comes as a festive interlude amid the terrible and wonderful events of Passiontide – events which thought and feeling can hardly bear to dwell upon. Can we really think and feel the crucifixion of the Son of God? Shall we be close to him when the sun is darkened and the very earth trembles and the ancient rocks are rent, and the tombs are opened? Yet, he calls us his friends, and seals that friendship in this sacred feast of his own body broken and his own blood outpoured. 'Take, eat and drink,' he bids us. He calls us his friends, who know what our master is about and share

MAUNDY THURSDAY SECOND SERMON

his purposes; shall we then be as slaves who run away and hide? In thought and feeling, we must watch with him, through the terrible darkness of this night of his betrayal – which is tonight liturgically, but which is also every night and every day in the history of mankind. We must watch with him, strong in the bond of charity, which bears all things, believes, hopes and endures. In mind and will, in reason and affection, we must even die with him, and rise again as new creations of his grace. 'From now on,' says St Paul, 'we judge no one by the standards of the world … If anyone is in Christ, he is a new creation; the old has passed away, behold the new has come.' Thus we drink his cup of agony, and find it is our cup of blessing.

'The charity of Christ compels us'; that charity, that friendship, must be our food and drink, the daily rations of our pilgrimage, our manna in the wilderness, the substance of our life of grace, and the faithful pledge of our risen life of glory. 'The charity of Christ compels us,' calls us, urges us, moves us, and transforms us.

In the mystical accents of the Song of Songs, the bridegroom calls his friends: 'Eat, my friends,' he says, 'and drink; drink deeply, dearest friends.'

Amen.

GOOD FRIDAY

Then Jesus took unto him the twelve, and said unto them, Behold, we go up to Jerusalem, and all things written by the prophets concerning the Son of Man shall be accomplished. For he shall be delivered unto the Gentiles, and shall be mocked and spitefully entreated and spitted on: and they shall scourge him, and put him to death; and the third day he shall rise again. And they understood none of these things, and this saying was hid from them; neither understood they the things which were spoken.

'Behold, we go up to Jerusalem' is the summons of this day. Behold, we go up to Jerusalem, to witness those things which come to pass here. We gaze and fix our minds and hearts upon the Passion of the Son of God. Behold, we go up to Jerusalem, to witness a mystery which astounds and stupefies, a mystery before which all words seem cheap, and every symbol seems too shallow. What thoughts, or what emotions can embrace such horrendous contradictions: the Son of God is spat on; the Son of God, the Word of life, goes down to death. How can we contemplate such things? How can we even begin to understand? How can we fix our minds and hearts on that?

GOOD FRIDAY

In the mystery of that moment, all the powers of heaven and earth and hell are shaken. The sun withholds its light, and the whole creation, which longs for its redemption, utters its astounded cry, as the earth quakes, and the rocks are rent. In that moment, all the hopes and expectations of religion are confounded, and the veil of the temple is rent in twain from the top unto the bottom. Many bodies of the saints arise and go about the city. That is to say, the whole settled order of the universe and of human life and expectations, all that is reasonable and dependable, is overturned, turned upside down when God, the Son of God, is spitted on, when the Word of life goes down to death.

How can we begin to understand this? On one side, we say it is the work of human wickedness, the pride of sin, which put to death the Son of God:

> Who was the guilty, who brought this upon thee?
> Alas, my treason, Jesu, hath undone thee.
> 'Twas, I, Lord Jesus, I it was denied thee.
> I crucified thee.

And that no doubt is true. And yet, how are we to believe that our paltry sins should overthrow the order of the universe, and dim the brightness of that infinite and everlasting glory which is God? Isn't it madness to suppose that God is in our hands?

> Alas, sweet lord, what were't to thee
> If there were no such worms as we?
> Heav'n ne'er the less still heav'n would be,
> Should mankind dwell
> In the deep hell.

THE SOUL'S PILGRIMAGE

What have his woes to do with thee?
Let him go weep
O'er his own wounds;
Seraphims will not sleep
Nor spheres let fall their faithful rounds.

Still would the youthful Spirits sing;
And still thy spacious palace ring.
Still would those beauteous ministers of light
Burn all as bright,

And bow their flaming heads before thee;
Still thrones and dominions would adore Thee;
Still would those ever-wakeful sons of fire
Keep warm thy praise
Both nights and days,
And teach thy lov'd name to their noble lyre.

Let froward dust then do its kind;
And give itself for sport to the proud wind.
Why should a piece of peevish clay plead shares
In the Eternity of thy old cares?
Why should'st thou bow thy awful breast to see
What mine own madnesses have done with me?

Will the gallant sun
E'er the less glorious run?
Will he hang down his golden head,
Or e'er the sooner seek his western bed,
Because some foolish fly
Grows wanton, and will die?

GOOD FRIDAY

> If I were lost in misery,
> What was it to thy heav'n and Thee?
> What was it to thy precious blood,
> If my foul heart call'd for a flood?

The power of human wickedness is no doubt great. Its machinations sink into the very fabric of our life and cripple the mind and heart. The power of human wickedness is great, but not so great that it should touch the holy peace of God, unless he willed that it should touch him. Jesus says to Pilate, 'Thou couldst have no power against me, unless it were given thee from above.' Human wickedness will raise itself in pride and claim to be 'as God', but that is devilish delusion. God is not touched unless he will it so to be.

We bear in mind today the weight of human wickedness, that reckless pride which rises up against the holiness of God and the order of his universe. But that is not what is first and most important in the mystery of the love of God, who freely wills our woes to touch his heart, who freely gives himself against our sins, in the sacrifice of Jesus Christ. That is the mystery of this day, and that is why we call this Friday 'Good'. We celebrate the mystery of the love of God: that 'God so loved the world, that he gave his only Begotten Son'. That is love unthinkable, utterly unmerited, beyond all possible expectation.

> For when we were yet without strength, in due time Christ died for the ungodly. For scarcely for a righteous man will one die: yet peradventure for a good man some would even dare to die. But God commendeth his love towards us, in that, while we were yet sinners, Christ died for us.

THE SOUL'S PILGRIMAGE

A beautiful seventeenth-century poem puts the message this way:

> My song is love unknown,
> My Saviour's love to me,
> Love to the loveless shown,
> That they might lovely be.
> O who am I,
> That for my sake
> My Lord should take
> Frail flesh, and die?

Our task today is nothing other than the contemplation of that mystery of love. It is to fix our minds and hearts upon the Passion and the dying of the Son of God. That is, in a way, the whole task of our discipleship. Christians often ask for detailed recipes for Christian life, solutions to all sorts of problems, great and small, and ways for dealing with our sins. All that is understandable. But in the end, there is only one answer to all of this: we must gaze upon the charity of God in Christ. The charity of God must be our food and drink. That is now our duty: to look upon the crucified, and that must become also our delight. We must be transformed by that renewal of our mind, so charity becomes the very substance of our souls.

This is why the heart of Christian life is the sacrament of Calvary, the sacrament of body broken, and blood outpoured. Christ's sacrifice abides with us in the sacrament, so that we may look upon the mystery of love and eat and drink the charity of God. Our misery and our shame is that we would contemplate all else but that. Surely, we must see that without charity, all else besides is nothing worth, 'sounding

GOOD FRIDAY

brass and tinkling cymbal, childish babble'. We must eat and drink the charity of God so that God's own charity, which hears, believes, hopes, and endures, may be the substance of our life and the renewal of our minds.

Amen.

EASTER DAY

*Of his own will, he brought us to birth,
by the word of truth; that we should be a kind of
first fruits of all his creation.*

Welcome, happy morning! age to age shall say;
   Hell today is vanquished! Heaven is won today!
Earth today confesses, clothing her for spring,
All good gifts return with her returning King;
Bloom in every meadow, leaves on every bough,
Speak his sorrows ended, hail his triumph now.

So sang Fortunatus, the great sixth-century Latin hymnographer, linking the feast of Jesus' resurrection with the glory of nature's resurgent springtime. And that is a connection which we, today – on this favoured island and in this gloriously decorated church – can hardly fail to make. Open the eyes of mind and heart: look and see. Look, and see, and understand. This is no idle demonstration: here and all about you is nature's parable of Jesus' resurrection, and nature's parable of our own new and risen life.

Springtime is the season of new life, after the dormancy and death of winter. A sleeping world awakens and rises up with new vitality. And the Church's Eastertide is the springtime of the spirit, the rising up from the icy grip of death to the vibrant warmth and light of resurrection. 'Awake thou that sleepest,

EASTER DAY

and arise from the dead, and Christ shall give thee light.'

In the cycle of nature's seasons, this is the time when we begin to plant our seeds. We bury them, deep down in the darkness, underground, where the new and tender shoots, nourished by sun and rain, will break through the rotting husks, and reach upward, to spread fresh leaves and blossoms in the light of day. That is nature's pattern of death and resurrection. Nature awakens to newness of life.

In all of this – in 'all this juice and all this joy', the poet Hopkins calls it – in all of this the scriptures teach us to read nature's parable of Easter. 'Unless a seed fall to the ground and die,' says Jesus, 'it abideth alone' – useless, unfruitful – 'but if it die, it bringeth forth much fruit.' St Paul expands upon that same parable: 'That which thou sowest, thou sowest not that body which shall be, but bare grain; it may chance of wheat, or of some other grain: but God giveth it a body as it hath pleased him, and to every seed its own body.'

Nature passes from death to life, in a travail of rebirth, dying, and rising to life again. It is a miracle, no doubt: it is the gift of God. But it is nevertheless, at the same time, a labour and a struggle. New birth is always a struggle, always a labour. T. S. Eliot, in a familiar line – now almost hackneyed, I'm afraid – says, 'April is the cruellest month, breeding lilacs from the dead land', and that thought too has its place in our parable. No new life, says Jesus, without the pains of travail. No Easter without Good Friday. So it was, so it is, and so it must be with our new life in Christ.

It is the gift of God; it is a miracle, yet it is not without the pains of travail. There must be a dying, a painful sloughing off of an old nature – a rotting husk; the old nature 'which is corrupt according to the deceitful lusts' – there must be a dying to old attitudes, old habits, old perspectives, and a putting on of a new nature, 'which

THE SOUL'S PILGRIMAGE

after God is created in righteousness and true holiness'.

Holy baptism is the sign and means and pledge of that new birth in us. We are baptized unto the death of Christ, that we might share his resurrection. The seed of Christ's risen life is sown in us. But that miracle of birth is only a beginning, just a starting point. There must be nutriment and training, a constant seeking of 'those things which are above.' There must be a shaping, a molding, and a pruning – often arduous and painful – of our affections and unruly wills, that 'our hearts may surely there be fixed where true joys are to be found'. 'Yea, I die daily,' says St Paul, 'I live, yet not I, but Christ liveth in me.'

There must be a conforming of our minds and hearts to the infinite and everlasting charity of God, shown to us in the dying of our saviour. 'Be not conformed to this present age,' says St Paul – do not be conformed to its standards and its attitudes, its principles and expectations – 'but be ye transformed, by the renewing of your mind', as newborn babes.

Easter is transformation: a transformation far beyond imagining. 'That which thou sowest, thou sowest not that body which shall be, but bare grain, it may chance of wheat or some other grain; but God giveth it a body as it hath pleased him.' The manner of God's life-giving transformation is beyond all explanation. We know not what we shall be, but we shall see our saviour as he is, and we shall be like him. God hath established resurrection in Christ, and what is Christ's, finally and everlastingly belongs to those who are his, for we are sons of God, by grace, and heirs of life eternal.

'See, beloved, see what manner of love the Father hath bestowed upon us, that we should be called the sons of God. And so we are.' And we look for the fulfilment of our sonship. For our citizenship is in heaven, from which we look for the

EASTER DAY

saviour, the Lord Jesus Christ: 'who shall change our vile body, that it may be fashioned like unto his glorious body, according to the working whereby he is able to subdue all things to himself.'

The Easter transformation is beyond all explanation and imagining. But, even here, the parable of nature would instruct us with a hint. As Dante puts it, in the *Paradiso*:

> I have seen the briar, a prickly thing
> All winter through;
> And on its tip, a rose at close of spring.

One final point: In the Gospel lesson for this morning's service, we have the story of St Mary Magdalene, with St Peter and St John, at the sepulchre of Jesus, bewildered because they could not find his body. The disciples went back home, but Mary stayed there weeping. And there she saw the risen Lord, and in the blindness of her tears mistook him for the gardener. But, you know, there is something strange and wonderful about Mary Magdalene's mistake. She thought he was the gardener. And surely, in a higher and deeper sense, that is precisely what he is: he is the gardener who sows the seed of new and risen life, deep down within the darkness of our hearts, who shapes and tends and nourishes that life in us with the Word of truth, with the everlasting charity of his own body broken and his own blood outpoured, to raise up soul and body unto life eternal.

Mary would cling to the earthly form of Jesus; but he says no, 'do not hold me'. Do not cling to earthly things. Rather, rise up; spring up; seek in faith your risen and ascended life in God, the everlasting life which is yours in Jesus Christ. Let nothing hold you back. Death is conquered! Man is free! Christ hath won the victory!

Amen.

EASTER MONDAY

But we trusted that it had been he which should have redeemed Israel.

Each of the four evangelists treats the events of the resurrection of Jesus somewhat differently, but they all give the impression that those events were unexpected, bewildering, and even dismaying to his followers. Occupied with mourning, trying to assimilate what seemed to them a tragedy, trying to accept the bitter end of all their cherished hopes, they had no eyes to see his resurrection. At first, they couldn't even recognize him. Mary Magdalene, weeping at the sepulchre, mistook him for the gardener. The disciples in Jerusalem, huddled together in an upper room, 'were terrified and affrighted, and supposed that they had seen a ghost'.

Most poignant of all those stories, I think, is the one we've just read as our Gospel lesson: the story of the two disciples walking on the road to Emmaus on Easter evening, sharing their sorrow with one another, and unable to recognize the stranger who joined them. That 'stranger' was Jesus. 'But their eyes were holden, that they should not know him.'

Some of you will remember, I'm sure, J. S. Bach's profound interpretation of that Emmaus story in his Cantata No. 6, for Easter Monday: *'Bleib bei uns'*. The opening strains of the first chorus unmistakeably recall the final chorus of the St John Passion, and express an intensity of grief, weariness,

EASTER MONDAY

and resignation altogether beyond words.

'But we trusted,' say the disciples, 'we trusted that it had been he which should have redeemed Israel.' Rumours of an empty tomb and an angelic message brought no renewal of hope but only bewilderment. Resurrection was simply not within the scope of their imagination or expectation. That Israel could be redeemed from worldly tyrannies was within the range of the possible; that Israel could be redeemed from sin and death was not. Only the light of Jesus' presence with them in Word and sacrament, only as he opened to them the scriptures, and was known to them in the breaking of bread; only then could they be carried beyond the settled and limited expectations of their own minds and hearts.

'We trusted that it had been he which should have redeemed Israel.'

Ah yes, but the true redemption of Israel is in the dying and rising again of the Son of God; a redemption far beyond their boldest dreams.

There were many aspects of Christian preaching which found ready acceptance in the ancient world, among both Jews and Greeks. St Paul, addressing the citizens of Athens, knew that he could call upon the testimony of the Greek poets: 'In God we live and move and have our being, as certain of your own poets have said.' But the apostolic preaching of the bodily resurrection was disconcerting. It seemed absurd. The Hellenistic world cried out for a 'spiritual' salvation, whereby immortal souls might escape from the prison of the body to a realm of pure spirit.

In the greatest literary work of Roman antiquity, the *Aeneid* of Virgil, there is a wonderful scene in which Aeneas, the hero, journeys through the underworld and meets the spirit of

THE SOUL'S PILGRIMAGE

Anchises, his father, in the Fields of Elysium. His father shows him a host of souls, gathered on the bank of a river, waiting to return from Paradise to earth. Aeneas cries out in protest:

> But, O my father, is it thinkable
> That souls could leave this blessedness, be willing
> A second time to bear the sluggish body,
> Trade paradise for earth?
> Alas, poor wretches, why such mad desire for light?

Anchises explains that only after drinking of the waters of the river Lethe, by which all memory is annulled, are the souls willing to enter bodily existence once again, the source of all the destructive passions of the soul – to enter once again into the conflict of body and soul, spirit and matter. Only in forgetfulness can it be borne.

The resurrection of Jesus was not a return to a mortal body. It was not resuscitation, as with Lazarus, or the widow's son at Nain, or Jairus' daughter; but neither was it the escape of immortal soul. It was the transformation of body, the reconciliation of flesh and spirit. The risen Lord was not a ghost: 'A spirit hath not flesh and bones as ye see me have.' The disciples were incredulous. Clearly, in spite of all that Jesus had said, they expected no such thing. They had hoped to embalm his body and preserve it as a sacred relic. Their immediate reaction to his resurrection was fear and dismay. After all, they knew the limits of the possible. 'Except I shall see in his hands the print of the nails, and put my finger into the print of the nails, and thrust my hand into his side, I will not believe,' said Thomas. But they did see, and they did believe, and their lives became witnesses to the resurrection.

But what does that witness mean? I think that for many

EASTER MONDAY

modern people, as for the ancients, the idea of resurrection seems disconcerting, not quite acceptable. We would accept more readily a more 'spiritual' salvation. People die, but their ideals live on. The flesh decays, but the human spirit is unconquerable. We live on in our posterity, and so on. But those supposedly spiritual immortalities have a terrible emptiness about them. As St Paul says to the Corinthians, 'If after the manner of men I have fought with beasts at Ephesus, what advantageth it me, if the dead rise not? Let us eat and drink, for tomorrow we die.' And I'm sure we all know the truth of these lines of Isaac Watts:

> Time, like an ever-rolling stream,
> Bears all its sons away;
> They fly, forgotten, as a dream
> Dies at the opening day.

The doctrine of the resurrection testifies to the wholeness of our salvation in Christ, the true redemption of Israel, in which nothing can finally be lost: nothing except sin. Our longing, says St Paul, is not to be unclothed, but to be 'clothed upon', to be reclothed, as Dante puts it in the *Paradiso:* 'reclothed in the holy and glorious flesh.' 'If Christ be in you,' says St Paul, 'The body is dead because of sin; but the spirit is life because of righteousness. But if the spirit of him who raised up Jesus from the dead dwell in you, he that raised up Christ from the dead shall also quicken your mortal bodies by the spirit that dwelleth in you.'

The manner of that quickening transformation is beyond all imagining. As St John says, 'we know not what we shall be, but we shall be like him.' God has established resurrection in Christ, and what is Christ's belongs to those who are his.

THE SOUL'S PILGRIMAGE

'For our citizenship is in heaven, from whence we look for the saviour, the Lord Jesus Christ; who shall change our vile body, that it may be fashioned like unto his glorious body, according to the working whereby he is able even to subdue all things unto himself.'

Amen.

EASTER I

They shall look upon me whom they have pierced.

No doubt this text from the prophet Zechariah would seem more appropriate to the darkness of Good Friday than to the glory of the Easter season. 'They shall look upon me whom they have pierced.' And yet, Good Friday is not just some tragic accident, reversed and cancelled out by the miracle of Easter; rather, as today's scripture lessons tell us, there is an intimate and necessary connection between the two, and we will not understand one without the other. The risen Lord appeared to his disciples and said to them: 'Peace be upon you. And when he had so said, he showed unto them his hands and his side.' The peace and forgiveness of which he speaks will not be understood apart from these sacred wounds. 'This is he who came by water and blood, even Jesus Christ' – this is he who came by the water and blood of crucifixion. 'They shall look upon me whom they have pierced.'

But just what are we to see when we look upon the crucified? What peace is there, what surety of forgiveness do we find in gazing on those wounds? The point is simply this: the wounds of Christ are the demonstration of the charity of God. The crucifixion of the Son of God, you see, is not just some tragic accident. On a certain level it is, of course, the work of human wickedness, and shows how far that wickedness can go;

THE SOUL'S PILGRIMAGE

but that is not the deepest truth of it. More profoundly, it is the demonstration of the charity of God: 'For God so loved the world that he gave his only Begotten Son.' He was wounded because he freely willed for it so to be.

What we see when we look upon the crucified is that charity of God, a charity which goes even down to death, and will not stop until it harrows hell itself. 'He descended into hell' says our Creed. Easter does not contradict Good Friday; rather, Easter is the declaration that the charity of God, which we see on Calvary, conquers hell itself; and is eternal life and resurrection. It is a charity which gives all, and therefore loses nothing.

> O all-sufficient sacrifice,
> Beneath thee hell defeated lies;
> Thy captive people are set free,
> And endless life restored in thee.

'They shall look upon me whom they have pierced.' We are to look upon this charity of God, lifted up upon the cross. 'As Moses lifted up the serpent in the wilderness, even so must the Son of Man be lifted up that whosoever believeth in him should not perish, but have eternal life.' The Son of Man is lifted up, that we may look upon, and believe the charity of God. We are to look upon and believe that charity, till it becomes the very substance of our minds and hearts, till it penetrates to every darkest corner of our dark souls and conquers every hell-bent force within us.

> Let holy charity
> Mine outward vesture be,

EASTER I

> And lowliness become mine inner clothing.
> Oh let it freely burn
> Till earthly passions turn
> To dust and ashes in its heat consuming;
> And let thy glorious light
> Shine ever on my sight
> And clothe me round, the while my path illuming.

We are to look upon and believe the charity of God in Jesus Christ and that is the beginning, the new birth and nutriment of charity in us. 'He that believeth in the Son of God hath the witness in himself; and this is the witness that God has given to us, eternal life; and this life is in his Son. He that hath the son hath life; and he that hath not the Son of God hath not life.' To know the charity of God is to overcome the world; 'and this is the victory that overcometh the world, even our faith', because faith knows the charity of God.

'As my Father hath sent me, even so send I you.' So says the risen Lord to his disciples. It is the office of the Church to believe the witness of the Son of God, and to have that witness in itself. That is to say, it is the office of the Church to look upon the charity of God, to declare and live that charity. That is the very substance of the sacraments we celebrate. In baptism, we celebrate that charity which calls us to be the Sons of God and heirs of life eternal; we celebrate the beginning, the new birth, of the life of faith. In the Eucharist, we celebrate the sacrifice of Christ, that the very charity of God may be our bread and wine, our food and drink. And that is the forgiveness of our sins.

But charity in us, it seems, is always only just begun. Easter in us, it seems, is only just begun. It is like a seed, planted deeply in the soil; the new life must break through the rotting husk, and

THE SOUL'S PILGRIMAGE

make its way toward the source of warmth and light. Our new birth is a struggle, certainly not without the pain of travail. How our sins and doubts oppress and weigh us down; how we waver and shilly-shally and even lose heart, how we wish there was just some simple, practical advice on how we should go about our task!

'They shall look upon me whom they have pierced.' There is simple, practical advice — perhaps, indeed, too simple for our taste: look upon the charity of God in Jesus Christ — don't fuss about your sins and wallow in your wretchedness; that is at best a useless occupation, and, at worst, a road to hell. It is the wrong focus of attention. Rather, look upon the charity of God, see the hands and side of Christ, and believe that charity which forgives your sins, and rejoice in life eternal. The devil doesn't really rule, and Easter scoffs at his pretensions.

Look upon the charity of God in Jesus Christ. Perhaps we don't see very clearly. 'Now, we see through a glass darkly,' says St Paul — we see as one might see a rather cloudy image in a mirror. But keep looking. Easter has begun in us. Spring has begun in us, and the new life will rise to bask in the warmth and light of God. 'Now we know in part, and prophesy in part, but then, we shall see face to face, and know even as we are known.'

Amen.

EASTER II

The Lord is my shepherd; therefore can I lack nothing.

In the scriptures of the Old Testament, the image of the shepherd is everywhere a symbol of divine government; and of human government, too, as an imitation of the divine. Thus God is addressed as shepherd: 'Hear, O thou shepherd of Israel, thou that leadest Joseph like a sheep.' And David, the shepherd boy, divinely anointed, becomes the shepherd king of Israel. And when Isaiah prophesies the coming deliverer, he too speaks of a shepherd: 'He shall lead his flock like a shepherd, and gather the lambs unto his bosom.' And when Jesus, offspring of the House of David, calls himself the 'good shepherd', his hearers would certainly have all this background in mind.

The image of the shepherd is a natural symbol of government. Not only in ancient Israel, but also in ancient Greece, it served this purpose. From the time of Homer, the Greeks spoke of kingship in terms of shepherding – a human office, no doubt, but also a reflection or imitation of the divine government of the universe. The image of the shepherd is a natural and universal symbol of divine and human government.

But there is a certain difficulty about the symbol. In the first book of Plato's dialogue called the *Republic*, there

THE SOUL'S PILGRIMAGE

is a conversation: Socrates is engaged in an argument with a Sophist called Thrasymachus on the subject of justice. At this particular point in the argument, they are discussing the art of government, and the idea of the shepherd is introduced. Thrasymachus accuses Socrates of naïve foolishness. 'You imagine,' he says, 'that a shepherd studies the interests of his flocks, tending them and fattening them up with some other end in view than his master's profit or his own; and so you don't see that, in politics, the genuine ruler regards his subjects exactly like sheep, and thinks of nothing else, night and days but the good he can get out of them for himself.' The gist of Socrates' reply is that, although there may indeed be false shepherds, it is the sole concern of the shepherd's art, as such, to do the best for the charges put under its care. Its own best interest is sufficiently provided for, so long as it does not fall short of all that shepherding should imply. On that principle, it follows, he says, that any kind of authority must, in its character of authority, consider solely what is best for those under its care.

Today, the second Sunday after Easter, is sometimes called 'Good Shepherd Sunday', because today's Gospel lesson draws a distinction between the good shepherd, who cares for the sheep, and the hireling, who is in the business for what he can get out of it for himself. 'I am the good shepherd,' says Jesus. 'The good shepherd giveth his life for the sheep.' Jesus' authority as shepherd, as governor of our lives, is established in his act of sacrifice: 'I lay down my life for the sheep.' And his shepherding is good indeed; his resurrection, our Easter joy, is our foretaste of the green pastures and still waters of eternal life.

'Yea, though I walk through the valley of the shadow of

death, I will fear no evil; for thou art with me; thy rod and thy staff comfort me.'

The idea of Jesus as the good shepherd is certainly a very attractive image, and it has inspired centuries of Christian devotion. And I suppose there is no passage in the whole of scripture better known or more loved than the twenty-third psalm, with its picture of divine shepherding. 'The Lord is my shepherd; therefore can I lack nothing. He shall feed me in green pastures and lead me forth beside the waters of comfort.' The image is almost too pretty: one can be sentimentally attached to the image, and altogether overlook the deeper levels of meaning it implies. It is fundamentally an image of the divine governing of the universe, the good shepherding of all things by God's wisdom and power.

In the earliest expressions of Christian art, the paintings which adorn the walls of the catacombs – those narrow labyrinthine tunnels which served as burial places in the early Christian centuries – a favourite theme is Jesus as the good shepherd. It is natural and obvious enough, of course, that the risen Lord should be represented as shepherd of the dead. 'Yea, though I walk through the valley of the shadow of death.' But it's not just that. Jesus is represented there as shepherd of the stars: the universal, cosmic shepherd, the Son of God – 'the power of God and the wisdom of God' – the good governor of all that is, shepherding all things to their appointed end.

The image of the good shepherd is fundamentally an image of divine government, an image of the universal providence of God in Christ. 'Other sheep I have, which are not of this fold; these also I must bring, and they should hear my voice; and there shall be one flock, and one shepherd.' It is a shepherding which includes the whole creation. As St Paul puts it in his Letter to the

THE SOUL'S PILGRIMAGE

Romans, 'the creation waits with eager longing for the revealing of the sons of God . . . because the creation itself will be set free from its bondage to decay, and obtain the glorious liberty of the children of God.'

The world has lots of hirelings, of course, who seem to be in it for what they can get out of it. It is easy enough to become cynical and doubtful about the divine government of things. The world is full of people exploiting one another, exploiting nature. But really, we need have no doubts on that score: God governs all things for the best. Jesus' resurrection is the ultimate witness of good shepherding: it witnesses to God's power to bring the highest good out of the worst evil. No doubt we have considerable capacities for wickedness; but it's just foolish presumption to suppose that our wickedness can have the last word. In the end, God's will is surely done.

That is the witness of the resurrection, and that is the promise of the resurrection. And that is the witness and promise of this sacrament we celebrate: out of body broken and blood shed, the grace of God brings new and eternal life.

'The wolf cometh, and the hireling fleeth,' but 'the good shepherd giveth his life for the sheep.' That is good shepherding, and with such shepherding, surely we lack nothing.

Amen.

EASTER III

*Ye shall be sorrowful, but your sorrow
shall be turned into joy.*

In the cycle of the Christian year, in the ancient lectionary – that cycle of Epistle and Gospel lessons which has served the church for well over a millennium and still survives in our *Book of Common Prayer* – the essential message of holy scripture, God's Word to us, is set before us in an orderly and supremely logical way. As we follow the lessons appointed for the Sundays and the great festivals, as we meditate upon them, as we open our minds and hearts to understand the pattern and meaning of them, we are led, step by step, into an ever deeper and clearer perception of Christian truth and the essentials of Christian life. What is involved in this is no arbitrary scheme for Bible reading, but a spiritual system, a design for sanctification, a coherent programme of practical spirituality.

Thus our scripture lessons for these Sundays after Easter speak to us not only about our saviour's resurrection, but also about the character of our own risen life in him. The Gospel lessons for the last three Sundays after Easter are all taken from St John's Gospel – from Jesus' discourse with his disciples at the Last Supper, one of the most beautiful and beloved passages of scripture, and full of the deepest theological significance. The three portions appointed for the Gospel lessons form a series. In today's lesson, Jesus warns his disciples about his departure

THE SOUL'S PILGRIMAGE

from them, and about the anguish that will involve. But there will be a purpose in that suffering, he tells them; it will be like the pains of travail, it will be the birth-pangs of a new form of life. 'Ye now therefore have sorrow,' he says, 'but your sorrow will be turned into joy.'

In next Sunday's Gospel reading, Jesus explains more precisely what that new form of life will be. 'If I go not away, the Comforter will not come unto you; but if I depart, I will send him unto you.' That is to say, the removal of the visible, bodily presence of God in Christ, his departure through death, resurrection, and ascension, would be the beginning of a new inner and spiritual relation to God.

And then, the Gospel lesson for the fifth Sunday speaks more fully of that inner spiritual relation to God in the life of prayer. 'The time cometh when I shall no more speak unto you in parables, but I shall show you plainly of the Father.' That is to say, no longer will it be a matter of knowing God by external things, by the visible, earthly presence of Jesus: God, who is Spirit, will be spiritually known and loved. Thus these three lessons set before us the essential meaning of the Easter season: suffering and resurrection, death and rebirth; they speak of transformation, an elevation from worldliness to new life in the Spirit. And thus, they prepare us to understand the meaning of Ascension and Pentecost.

That is the general pattern and argument of these lessons. But today we must concern ourselves more particularly with the details of today's lesson. 'Ye shall be sorrowful,' says Jesus, 'but your sorrow shall be turned into joy.' Think for a moment about the context of these words, at the Last Supper. It was an occasion of high tragedy: the powers of darkness were fast closing in; Judas had already gone out to betray him. 'And it was night.' All that remained was to prepare the faithful band for the terrors of the morrow. 'Ye now therefore have sorrow.' Sorrow indeed. Not only the sadness of a final farewell of friends; but the hopeless sorrow of the death of every hope and every good expectation. 'We trusted that it had been he who should have redeemed Israel.' Not just a discouraging incident, not just a great disappointment, but the end of all hope: the very sun would be darkened, and the foundations of the earth would quake.

In that context, the words of Jesus must have seemed very strange indeed: 'What is this that he saith, a little while? We cannot tell what he saith.' What is this talk of departure and return, of sorrow being turned into joy? 'We cannot tell what he saith.' Jesus spoke of his going to the Father: 'Now I go my way to him that sent me, and none of you asketh me, "Whither goest thou?" But because I have said these things unto you, sorrow hath filled your heart. Nevertheless, I tell you the truth; it is expedient for you that I go away: for if I go not away, the Comforter will not come unto you; but if I depart, I will send him unto you.'

They would have sorrow, he told them: but it would not be a barren, empty sorrow. 'A woman, when she is in travail, hath sorrow, because her hour is come: but as soon as she is delivered of the child, she remembereth no more the anguish, for joy that a man is born into the world.' Sorrow with a purpose: No new life without suffering, says Jesus. And so it must be with the disciples. Only when their limited hopes and ambitions were shattered in the darkness of doubt and despair would they give birth to the new life of faith. Only when they had learned the radical insufficiency of their old nature could they find their true sufficiency in the enabling divine Spirit,

THE SOUL'S PILGRIMAGE

the Comforter. Only then would they learn to know God as Spirit. 'If I go not away, the Comforter will not come unto you.' That shattering, that sorrow, would be the precondition of true joy.

Thus Jesus explained his departure, and foretold their sorrow. But to explain sorrow is not in any measure to mitigate the reality of the experience when it comes. If the explanation is remembered at all, it seems rather cold comfort. So it was with the disciples. The death and resurrection of Jesus was not for them an immediate occasion of joy, but of fear. They did not – could not – see the point of it all. They were afraid. They could not even find his body. They ran away and hid. But, as Jesus had promised, their sorrow, this fear, this bewilderment, this shattering of natural hopes and natural sufficiency was not pointless. It was only through all this that the disciples were able to know the risen Christ, and to receive a new sufficiency of knowledge and action in the presence of God's Spirit. 'He will lead you into all truth.' 'He will show you things to come.' All the sorrow was as pains of travail – out of it came new life, a new kingdom of the Spirit, a new world.

What was true for those first disciples is true also for all who would be Christians. We who would be risen with Christ must heed his admonition: No new life without the pains of travail. 'In the world ye shall have tribulation,' and that is not just an unfortunate accident: it is part of our dying with Christ. It is only thus that our salvation is worked out – 'like as silver, which from the earth is tried, and purified seven times in the fire.' Only in that refinement is the Spirit's gift realised in us. In the perspective of God's providence, in the pattern of salvation, sorrow and fear and doubt are not just unfortunate accidents; they are elements in God's fitting us for glory.

EASTER III

Christ's wounds are the signs of his glory, and so must ours be.

This liturgy we celebrate this morning is our constant reminder that the signs of body broken and blood shed are the signs of the risen Lord, and new life in the Spirit. 'Be of good cheer,' says Jesus, 'I have overcome the world.'

'Your sorrow will be turned into joy.'

Amen.

EASTER IV
FIRST SERMON

It is expedient for you that I go away.

The Gospel lessons for the last three Sundays after Easter are all taken from the sixteenth chapter of St John's Gospel from Jesus' discourse with his disciples at the Last Supper. That discourse is one of the most beautiful and most beloved passages of scripture, and full of the deepest and most important theological significance. The three portions of it chosen for the Gospel lessons on these three Sundays form a series. In last Sunday's lesson, Jesus warns his followers about his departure from them, and all the suffering that it will involve. But there will be a purpose in that suffering, he tells them; it will be like the pains of travail, it will be the birth pangs of a new form of life. 'Ye now therefore have sorrow,' he says, 'but your sorrow shall be turned into joy.'

In today's Gospel lesson, Jesus explains more precisely what that new form of life will be: 'If I go not away, the Comforter will not come unto you; but if I depart, I will send him unto you.' That is to say, the removal of the visible, bodily presence of God in Christ, his departure through death, resurrection, and ascension, though it would be for his disciples a great sorrow, would be the beginning of a new inner and spiritual relation to God.

Next Sunday's lesson speaks more fully of that inner and

EASTER IV FIRST SERMON

spiritual relation to God, the life of prayer. 'The time cometh when I shall no more speak unto you in parables, but I shall show you plainly of the Father.' That is to say, no longer will it be a matter of knowing God just by way of external things, by way of the visible and earthly presence of Jesus. God, who is Spirit, will be spiritually known and loved.

Thus these three lessons, taken as a series, set before us the essential meaning of the Easter season: they speak of suffering and resurrection; they speak of death and rebirth; they speak of a transition – an elevation – from worldliness to new life in the Spirit.

That is the general argument and meaning of these Gospel lessons; but today, we must concern ourselves more particularly with the details of today's lesson. 'It is expedient for you that I go away,' Jesus says, 'for if I go not away, the Comforter will not come unto you; but if I depart, I will send him unto you.' 'Comforter' is a rather old-fashioned word. What it means is 'strengthener' or 'fortifier'; it is a name for the Holy Spirit. So what Jesus is telling his disciples is that only by his own departure will they be able to know the presence of God and Holy Spirit. So long as he was physically present with them, they would continue to be related to him in worldly ways. They would be related to him as a great teacher, a national leader, a great hero and wonder-worker, and so on. Only by Jesus' departure would that relation be purified to become a purely spiritual relation. 'If I depart, I will send him unto you.'

Then Jesus goes on to speak of the effects of that new spiritual relation: 'When he is come he will reprove the world of sin, and of righteousness, and of judgement: of sin, because they believe not on me; of righteousness, because I go to my Father, and ye see me no more; of judgement, because the prince of this world is judged.' To know God as Spirit is to have a new and

THE SOUL'S PILGRIMAGE

different standpoint; sin and righteousness and judgement are no longer seen in terms of worldly standards and conventions and authorities. Sin is essentially unbelief – a turning away from the revealed truth; righteousness is essentially obedience to that truth, and the basis of judgement is no longer a worldly standard – 'the prince of this world is judged'. The Holy Spirit, 'the Spirit of truth' is the living guide to all truth.

The passage concludes by setting all this within the context of God's own life. 'He (the Spirit) shall glorify me: for he shall receive of mine and shall show it unto you. All things that the Father hath are mine: therefore said I, that he shall take of mine, and shall show it unto you.' Father, Son and Spirit are one God. To know God as life-giving Spirit is not to know some other God; it is to know God as Father, and God as Son, ever more perfectly in a spiritual way.

By these lessons, Jesus, at the Last Supper, prepared his followers to understand the meaning of his Passion, Resurrection, and Ascension, and prepared them to receive the Spirit's gift at Pentecost. And for us, these lessons have the same significance, as we too share in those events. 'It is expedient for you that I go away,' says Jesus. Our worldly attachments are very strong, and the temptation is always strong to regard our religion as just another aspect of those worldly attachments – to make religion serve the world and our worldly interests. But Jesus departs from us, and we must find him spiritually, or not at all.

It is in this sense that our worldly tribulations may be altogether salutary: by the harsh disciplines of disappointment and bewilderment and sorrow we may learn to find our treasure elsewhere, and our sorrow may be turned to joy.

Amen.

EASTER IV
SECOND SERMON

Let every one be swift to hear, slow to speak, slow to wrath; for the wrath of man worketh not the righteousness of God.

Our text comes from today's Epistle lesson, from the Epistle of St. James; and in that lesson, St James seems, perhaps, at first, to be dealing in clichés or platitudes; points which seem perfectly obvious, and to be taken for granted. 'Every good gift and every perfect gift is from above,' he tells us; surely there is nothing very novel in that thought. Surely, that is a truth which wise men and women, at all times, and in all places, have always recognized. St Paul, in Acts 17, was able to quote the pagan Greek poets on the subject: 'In God we live, and move, and have our being; as some of your own writers have said, "we are all his children".'

God is 'the Father of lights,' says St James, 'with whom is no variableness, neither shadow of turning.' God is the unfailing source of all life and every blessing. Behind all the changes and vicissitudes of nature and human life, his purpose abides, sure and steadfast, eternally just, eternally good. 'Every good and perfect gift is from above, and cometh down from the Father of lights.' That is God's eternal providence, and the knowledge of that providence is the sure ground of all spiritual life. Boethius,

THE SOUL'S PILGRIMAGE

that great sixth-century Christian poet, from the depths of worldly tribulation, says it beautifully in his prayer:

> Grant, Father, to my mind that I may rise
> To thy majestic seat;
> Grant me to gaze upon the fountain of the good,
> To fix the clear sight of my mind on thee.
> Disperse the clouds and heaviness of earth,
> And shine forth in thy splendour.
> For to the blessed, thou art serenity and rest;
> To see thee is their end and their beginning,
> At once their mover and their leader,
> At once their pathway, and their good.

Perhaps all that seems obvious enough; there is nothing very novel about it. But it is, nevertheless, a point which Christians in our own time would do well to hold quite firmly in mind. God's justice, God's righteousness, is eternal and unchanging, unswayed through all of our perversities and all our aberrations. And in the end, God's will is done. That truth of God's eternal providence is fundamental truth, at the very basis of all spiritual life; and we forget it, or neglect it at our peril.

But St James has something more in mind, something quite beyond what wise men always and everywhere have known: 'Of his own will he brought us to birth by the word of truth, that we should be a kind of first-fruits of all creation.' He points us to the saving work of God in Christ, the word Incarnate, 'the implanted word; which is able to save your souls.' And the Gospel lesson for today speaks of our receiving of that 'perfect gift' – 'the implanted word' – in the power of the Spirit, 'the Comforter,' 'the Spirit of Truth' – the gift of the Risen and Ascended Lord.

EASTER IV SECOND SERMON

By the 'perfect gift' of the divine Spirit, we are 'a kind of first-fruits of all creation'. God's creation has a spiritual purpose, a spiritual end, of which we are 'a kind of first-fruits', a beginning of the harvest. As we are born anew by the gift of God's Spirit, as we share consciously and lovingly in God's eternal purpose, his will for his creation becomes manifest in us. In us, dumb nature finds the voice of praise and adoration. In and through the worship of Almighty God, the whole creation, groaning until now in pains of travail, awaiting its redemption, begins to find its destiny. In that sense, we who are born of the Spirit are the first-fruits of all creation, the beginning of the harvest.

'Ye know this, my beloved brethren,' says St James, 'and so let everyone be swift to hear, slow to speak, slow to wrath; for the wrath of man worketh not the righteousness of God.' Knowing the steadfast providence of God, and the gracious work of Christ for our salvation, we must receive, with meekness, his word implanted in our minds and hearts: with meekness, with awe-filled adoration, humility and patience. Such virtues as meekness, humility and patience, are perhaps not very prominent in the modern Christian's armoury. There is so much that seems so obviously wrong in our world; so much wrong in the Church; so much wrong in us; so much to be done: how can we afford patience and meekness?

'Be swift to hear,' says St James, 'Receive with meekness the implanted word which is able to save your souls.' God's will for our salvation will not be served by frantic speech and wrathful deeds. So busy and distracted by what seem to us obvious goods; swift in speech, swift in wrath, we become inattentive to God's word – slow to hear. We become distracted in the pursuit of a myriad of apparently excellent gifts, and fail in our perception of that perfect gift which is ours for the listening. 'Be swift to hear.'

Thus, today's Collect would have us pray for patient attentiveness to God's word; for God alone can order our unruly wills and affections. We pray that we may love his commandments, and desire what he promises; that our wills may be steadfast, in accord with the eternal and invariable righteousness of God; that amid 'the sundry and manifold changes of the world', amid all the distractions of swift speech and swift wrath, 'our hearts may surely there be fixed where true joys are to be found'.

The message of the Easter season, and the lessons of this Sunday, are simple and vitally important. The perfect gift of God, the seed of new spiritual life, the word of God, the seed of resurrection, has been implanted in our minds and hearts. In Eastertide, we celebrate the Passover of Christ, through death to resurrection; and that must be our Passover as well: 'Ye are dead, and your life is hid with Christ in God.' The temple of his body must be raised up in us, the house of God must be rebuilt in us and among us: not in frantic speech and wrathful deeds, but in attentiveness to God's word, in steady, constant discipline of prayer, in patient and long-suffering labour of mind and heart and hands, waiting upon the Spirit's strengthening, in the sure and certain confidence that though we be in sorrow for a season, the good and perfect gifts of God our Father do not fail. Fear not; it is your Father's pleasure to give you a kingdom. And he will surely do it.

Amen.

EASTER V
ROGATION

The creation waits with eager longing for the revealing of the sons of God... because the creation itself will be set free from its bondage to decay, and obtain the glorious liberty of the children of God. We know that the whole creation has been groaning in travail together until now; and not only the creation, but we ourselves who have the first fruits of the Spirit, groan inwardly as we wait for adoption as sons, the redemption of our bodies.

This fifth Sunday after Easter is commonly called Rogation Sunday, because it immediately precedes the three Rogation days and it is about the significance of the Rogation days that I intend to speak. And I should like us to think especially of the connection between Rogation and Easter.

The word 'Rogation' means 'asking' – in this context, asking in the sense of Prayer – and the Rogation days are days of solemn prayer. The observance of them dates back at least to the fourth century, and have always been particularly associated with the blessing of the fields and the newly sown crops. One of the traditional ceremonies is the singing of the litany by priest and congregation as they go in procession through the fields around the boundaries of the parish – a ceremony which is still observed in some parishes in rural areas.

THE SOUL'S PILGRIMAGE

Thus, Rogationtide has to do with the relation between man and God and Nature – and that is a relation which seems to become increasingly obscure in an increasingly urban society – where people's dependence upon nature becomes less obvious; where milk seems to be produced from paper cartons, and spinach seems to grow in plastic bags; 'And all is seared with trade,' says the poet, Hopkins, 'bleared, smeared with toil; And wears man's smudge and shares man's smell: the soil/Is bare now, nor can feet feel, being shod'.

Our remarkable technology has enabled us to bring nature into considerable subjection. If the mountain is in the way, we can move it, if the climate is too severe, we can produce a controlled environment; we can travel across the continent, or around the world, without ever stepping on a blade of grass. We can harness the winds, and even the mighty tides of the ocean can be made to serve us – perhaps.

It is true that our mastery is incomplete; we make mistakes, sometimes disastrous ones, and sometimes the forces of nature seem to wreak vengeance upon us; but surely nevertheless, we have come a very long way in fulfilling our Creator's mandate that we should have dominion over nature.

> God said, let them have dominion over the fish of the sea, and over the birds of the air, and over the cattle, and over all the earth, and over every creeping thing that creepeth upon the earth... and it was so.

We have come a very long way in the exercise of our dominion; there are not many frontiers left. But the result of our dominion presents us now with many and agonizing dilemmas: for it seems that our exploitation of nature has inevitable and rather

EASTER V

unwelcome limits. It seems that we have problems other than those of improving our techniques of exploitation.

The season of Rogationtide invites us to consider just what human dominion over nature should mean: to consider whether, in truth, human exploitation of it is the meaning and end of nature. Rogationtide invites us to consider a very different view of the matter, according to which the meaning and end of creation is the service and praise of God. Perhaps you recall, for instance, St Francis of Assisi's glorious 'Canticle of the Sun', paraphrased in one of our hymns, in which 'Brother Sun' and 'Sister Moon' and all the elements of nature are called to praise God:

> Dear mother earth, who day by day
> Unfoldest blessings on our way,
> O Praise Him, Alleluia
> Thou flowing water pure and clear
> Make music for the Lord to hear.
> O Praise Him, Alleluia.

The meaning and the end of nature is the praise of God, and human dominion over nature has to do with bringing nature to that fulfilment. Man, as a unity of spirit and matter, is a kind of mediator between God and nature. Humanity is nature's priest in bringing the created order to redemption. That vocation is wonderfully symbolized in the offertory of our liturgy, where the grains of wheat gathered from the fields and made into bread, and the grapes brought in from the hillsides and made into wine, become the elements of the sacrifice of praise; we lift them up.

Eastertide is about change and transformation – about the

THE SOUL'S PILGRIMAGE

elevation of life to a new level of spirit. And all nature has its part in Easter – for the whole creation groans in travail, awaiting redemption.

In and through the redeemed spirit of humanity, dumb nature is to find a voice – the voice of praise – the stones, the wood and the metal must learn the harmony of God's praise – chaotic sound must find the form of music to praise him.

As Paul Claudel, the great twentieth-century French poet and diplomat, summed it up: 'Everything that the redemptive has brought forth must in the end hear also the Redemptive word, that nothing in his creation be stranger to his revelation in glory.' 'The creation waits with eager longing for the revealing of the sons of God because the creation itself will be set free from its bondage to decay and obtain the glorious liberty of the children of God.'

The point of Rogation, now at the conclusion of Eastertide, is that the whole creation, the whole order of nature be brought into the liturgy of the resurrection.

Amen.

ASCENSION

*Ye men of Galilee, why stand ye gazing
up into heaven?*

The Gospel lessons for the last three Sundays after Easter – all of them from the sixteenth chapter of St John – prepare us to see and understand the meaning of our Lord's Ascension. Those lessons are all about his departure and return.

> Now I go away to him that sent me, and none of you asketh me, Whither goest thou? But because I have said these things unto you, sorrow hath filled your heart. Nevertheless, I tell you the truth; it is expedient for you that I go away: for if I go not away, the Comforter will not come to you; but if I depart, I will send him unto you.

Thus Jesus spoke to his disciples, and they did not understand: 'What is this that he saith unto us, "A little while and ye shall not see me; and again a little while and ye shall see me; and, Because I go to the Father?" They said therefore, "What is this that he saith, A little while? We cannot tell what he saith."' Can't you taste the bewilderment, the pain and sad confusion in those words, 'We cannot tell what he saith?' They did not see how they could do without the presence of their friend and leader: how could his departure be expedient for them? And what could he possibly mean by promising another 'Comforter'?

THE SOUL'S PILGRIMAGE

'We cannot tell what he saith.'

And now, at his Ascension, still they are bewildered and confused, and stand gazing up into heaven. And, 'behold, two men stood by them in white apparel' – two angelic messengers – 'which also said, "Ye men of Galilee, why stand ye gazing up into heaven? This same Jesus, which is taken up from you into heaven, shall so come in like as ye have seen him go into heaven".'

Departure and return: but only at Pentecost did they begin to understand the meaning of these things. Jesus had promised them, 'When the Comforter is come, whom I will send unto you from the Father, even the Spirit of truth, which proceedeth from the Father, he shall testify of me: and ye also shall bear witness, because ye have been with me from the beginning.' Only then would all these things, the experience of God's presence with them, begin to make sense. And only then could they be witnesses, going out into all the world to preach the Gospel to every creature.

So it was with the disciples: 'We cannot tell what he saith'; and they stood bewildered and confused, 'gazing up into heaven'. And how, I wonder, is it with us? Do we know 'what he saith'? Departure and return – these great festivals of Ascension and Pentecost, what do they really mean to us? And what practical significance do they have for our life as Christians here and now? These festivals represent the most profound, and at the same time most elementary lessons of Christian spiritual life; but can we even begin to grasp what they mean? Can we 'tell what he saith', or must we stand gazing – bewildered and confused – gazing up into heaven, looking towards spiritual reality, some home of the spirit which can never be ours, and living our lives as though Ascension and Pentecost had never really happened for us?

What does the Ascension really mean? Remember that incident in the Easter Garden, when Magdalene longs to

ASCENSION

embrace the risen Lord? And he says, 'Touch me not, for I am not yet ascended to the Father.' The point is this: those who would follow him must be weaned from earthly hopes and expectations. The earthly, the fleshly, must be transformed, transfigured, so that we see its true reality as spiritual. In that sense he must depart from us, and it is expedient that he go away. 'The flesh profiteth nothing,' he tells us, 'the words I speak unto you, they are spirit, and they are life.' In the travail of earthly life, we must give birth to faith – a faith which knows God as Spirit. And thus, he returns to us in the power of the Spirit, and that is Pentecost.

I know that to speak of spiritual life, or life in the Spirit, sounds pretty obscure to many Christians. But if that is really so, what then is our religion all about? 'We have not followed cunningly devised fables,' says St Peter. We are risen with Christ – we are born anew of water and the spirit, we seek those things which are above. The life of Ascension and Pentecost is the fundamental reality of our life: we are to ascend with him 'in heart and mind' and 'with him continually dwell'. And that is not really so obscure. There is a fine picture of spiritual life set before us, for instance, in today's Epistle lesson, in terms which everyone can understand:

> The end of all things is at hand; be ye therefore sober, and watch unto prayer. And above all things have fervent charity among yourselves: for charity shall cover the multitude of sins. Use hospitality one to another without grudging. As every man hath received the gift, even so minister the one to another, as good stewards of the manifold grace of God. If any man speak, let him speak as the oracles of God: if any minister, let him do it as of the ability which God giveth;

THE SOUL'S PILGRIMAGE

that God in all things be glorified through Jesus Christ, to whom be praise and dominion for ever and ever.

'The end of all things is at hand.' In Ascension and Pentecost, the end of all things – the life of heaven, the point, the meaning, the conclusion of all things – is indeed at hand. Therefore, be sober, be serious – don't just stand there gazing up into heaven. The spiritual life of God's kingdom is yours – here in your midst, within your grasp, within you. Therefore, watch unto prayer, and above all, have fervent charity among yourselves, for that is to live the spiritual life of heaven here on earth.

As Edward Pusey, a great nineteenth-century Anglican preacher, puts it in his sermon for the Ascension:

> O choose ye then, on this Great Day, if ye have not yet chosen; if ye have, in the light of that Heaven which your Saviour this day opened for you, opens to you, pray ye Him to bind your choice by the bonds of His Everlasting Love. Let not this great sight fade from your eyes. Let not the tinsel of the world dazzle the eyes which were formed to 'see the King in His Beauty.' Let not the praise of men dull the ears, which were formed to hear the Blissful Words 'well done faithful servant.' Let not cares, riches, pleasures of this world, choke the heart, which was formed to contain the love of God. Pray, and all is thine. Thine is God Himself, who teacheth thee to pray for Himself. To pray is to go forth from earth, and to live in Heaven. Learn to commend thy daily acts to God, so shall the dry every-day duties of common life be steps to Heaven and lift thy heart thither; commend thyself to God in moments of leisure, so shall thy rest be rest in God, and conduct thee to thine Everlasting Rest. He, thy

ASCENSION

Head, is Above; shall the heart be any more below?

'Ye men of Galilee, why stand ye gazing up into heaven?'
Heaven is yours; lay hold upon it.
'Be sober, and watch unto prayer.'

Amen.

SUNDAY AFTER ASCENSION

That which is born of the Spirit is spirit.

The great festival of the Ascension of Christ seems to be a difficult one for modern Christians, perhaps even a little embarrassing. We know perfectly well, after all, that God is not really seated up there in some place called 'heaven,' above the sky. God is pure spirit, equally in all places and all times, and equally beyond all places and times. Even a place beyond the sky won't do. So all the Ascensiontide language about Christ ascending into the clouds perhaps sounds more appropriate to a fairy-story than to serious theology. Consequently, modern theologians sometimes try to substitute a new language, from the field of depth psychology, or some other source. But the advantages of the new language are dubious. To say that God is the mysterious ground of self-consciousness is no doubt somehow true, but it is probably no more generally illuminating than to say that God is above the sky.

Perhaps we do better simply to acknowledge that any language we use must be language which belongs to our earthly experience, and therefore cannot apply literally to God. That is a fact of which the ancient theologians were always perfectly aware. So perhaps we might as well stick fundamentally to the old familiar images, employed by the scriptures, and try to

SUNDAY AFTER ASCENSION

understand the sense of them before we try casting about for new, improved versions. We can easily make new Prayer Books, of course, or even new Bibles; but before we undertake such ventures, and tamper with matters so basic to our spiritual health, we had better be very sure what we're talking about and what we expect to gain in the attempt.

The scriptures tell us that Jesus ascended into the heavens, and the Church celebrates that event as a great festival. What does it mean? To begin with, the ascension is an historical fact, just as the birth and death and resurrection of Jesus are historical facts. It is an historical fact, witnessed to by those 'men of Galilee' who were left gazing up into the sky – no doubt greatly astonished – as a cloud received the risen Christ out of their sight. As a fact, it is no more doubtful than any of the other facts about Jesus. So our question is not really whether it happened, but why it happened, and why it happened in this way.

The Gospel lessons for the last few Sundays after Easter go a long way towards explaining the ascension, because in those lessons Jesus tells his disciples why he must go away. 'It is expedient for you that I go away,' he tells them, 'for if I go not away, the Spirit will not come to you.' That is to say, they would cling to his earthly form as long as they could. 'But if I depart, I will send him unto you.'

The risen Lord ascends from the realm of the flesh to the realm of the spirit, and it is precisely that movement – from flesh to spirit – which is represented in the fact of the ascension. His flesh transformed in resurrection, he returns to that realm of spirit whence he came. As the Epistle to the Ephesians puts it, 'Now that he ascended, what is it but that he also descended first into the lower parts of the earth? He that descended is the

THE SOUL'S PILGRIMAGE

same also that ascended up far above all heavens, that he might fill all things.' Or, as Jesus himself says, in St John's Gospel, 'No man hath ascended up to heaven, but he that came down from heaven, even the Son of Man which is in heaven.'

So, Jesus returns to that realm of spirit whence he came, and he tells us that by so doing he will send us the Spirit.

The point is that he takes humanity – his humanity and our humanity – back to that realm of spirit to which it belongs and endows it with spiritual life. As an ancient hymn puts it,

> Yea angels tremble when they see
> How changed is our humanity;
> That flesh hath purged what flesh had stained,
> And God, the flesh of God, hath reigned.

That was indeed the whole point of his coming: to rescue us from our worldliness and restore to us our true spiritual destiny as sons of God. As some of the ancient Church Fathers were fond of saying, 'God became man, that men might become gods.' 'Wherefore he saith, when he ascended up on high, he led captivity captive, and gave gifts unto men.' And it is, of course, the outpouring of those spiritual gifts which we celebrate in the great feast of Pentecost next week.

Thus the Ascension of Christ proclaims and celebrates our spiritual destiny as sons of God. 'That which is born of the flesh is flesh,' Jesus tells Nicodemus, 'and that which is born of the Spirit is spirit.' We are born of the Spirit, and therefore we are spirit; and spirit cannot ultimately be limited by worldly ends and earthly limitations. By the comfort – by the strengthening, transforming power – of the Holy Spirit of God, we are to be exalted 'unto the same place whither our saviour Christ is gone

SUNDAY AFTER ASCENSION

before'. That is to say, we belong to that same spiritual realm — not literally a place, of course, but a condition of life — to which the ascended Christ belongs.

This fact should be of the most vital concern to each one of us: we are sons of God, born of the spirit with a spiritual destiny. I know that this is a difficult point, but I'm sure it's crucially important that we consider it carefully, and I wish that I could say it better. It seems to me such a pity that for so many professing Christians, our religion seems basically only a moral code, rules for decent living, solutions to world problems, and so on, while the cultivation of the spirit is regarded as something extra, something for the few who are good at prayer and meditation, and such things. Certainly, all these things, are important: our moral life is always desperately in need of attention, and world problems are so formidable that it's painful even to think about them. I'm not suggesting for a moment that we should ignore these things, even if we could. But surely the attitude, the orientation, which puts them first, is all wrong.

For us as Christians, the good we can do in this world, the good we can do for ourselves and for one another, springs from, is part of, and is nourished by, our spiritual orientation. It is that spiritual orientation, that habitual practice of referring all things to their end in God, that ascension 'in heart and mind' which is the essence of our religion; and it is that truth which the feast of the Ascension proclaims.

'That which is born of the Spirit is spirit,' says Jesus. We are born of the Spirit, and therefore we are spirit. And because we are spirit, we turn towards our spiritual home, that realm of the Spirit 'whither our saviour Christ is gone before'. That realm of the Spirit, is the eternal life of God himself. It is that high destiny which our faith must keep ever fresh before our eyes.

THE SOUL'S PILGRIMAGE

As Bishop Wordsworth's Ascensiontide hymn expresses it (with perhaps indifferent poetry, but certainly with sound doctrine):

> He has raised our human nature
> On the clouds to God's right hand;
> Where we sit in heavenly places,
> There with him in glory stand.
> Jesus reigns, adored by angels,
> Man with God is on the throne;
> Mighty Lord in thine Ascension
> We by faith behold our own.

Amen.

PENTECOST/ WHITSUNDAY

God is a Spirit: and they that worship him must worship him in spirit and in truth.

He that hath my commandments and keepeth them, he it is that loveth me.

All those devout Jews, gathered from every corner of the ancient Mediterranean world to celebrate the feast of Pentecost in Jerusalem, must have been greatly shocked by the behaviour of the disciples of Jesus, described in today's lesson from the Acts of the Apostles. Quite a display, really. Some of the bystanders, inclined to scoff, decide that the disciples must be drunk – so early in the day, too; only the third hour! But others were able to discern that this was not drunken babbling, but the inspiration of which the prophets had spoken; that inspiration by which the young would see visions, and the old would dream dreams. These others, even if they knew no Aramaic, understood the essential meaning of this ecstatic speech. The spirit of the Lord had taken possession: had filled the whole house where they were sitting, and now spilled out into the world.

The Feast of Pentecost, the Feast of Weeks, for which the crowds had gathered, fifty days after the Passover, commemorates chiefly the giving of the law of the covenant to Moses on Mount Sinai, when 'The whole of Mount Sinai was covered with smoke,

THE SOUL'S PILGRIMAGE

because the Lord had come down on it in fire …'. Now there was a new Pentecost, a new covenant, a new law, given again with torrents of fire: not now the fire of judgement: 'the sudden Torrent's dread', but now the fire of love 'resting on each one of them'. And now, mankind's ancient disobedience, represented by the division of tongues – the confusion of human speech with the destruction of the tower of Babel – is healed; and the inspiration of the spirit unites devout people out of every nation under heaven. 'We hear them speak in our own tongue the wonderful works of God.' The new Pentecost establishes the new covenant, the new spiritual kingdom that Jesus had promised.

Over and over again in the history of the Church there have been attempts to recover the experience of Pentecost. Remember how Simon Magus, in the Acts of the Apostles, tried to buy the experience from the disciples, and ever since we use the word 'simony' to refer to commercial trafficking in spiritual gifts. In the second century, Tertullian and his Montanist followers thought that the pentecostal experience was the one true mark of the Christian Church, and the necessary condition of Christian life, and so they separated themselves from the general body of believers who had not that experience.

As we know from St Paul's Epistles, there were Christians in the early Church who thought it their vocation to recover the ecstasy of Pentecost, to imitate it, to repeat the experience. 'They spoke with tongues and caused wonder.' And there are modern Christians, too, who have the same idea. But as St Paul explained, the experience of ecstasy is not really the point; as for himself, he says, he'd rather speak a few intelligible words: 'I will speak with the Spirit,' he says, 'and I will speak with the understanding also.'

PENTECOST/WHITSUNDAY

The Spirit's work is not just ecstasy: religion is not just experience. Ecstasy requires interpretation. The Spirit's inspiration expresses itself in ordered forms. As in the first creation, the Spirit brooded over chaos, forming it, so in the new creation of Pentecost, the Spirit brings forth form and order; not just ecstasy, but lucid words and works of beauty and charity. Inspiration is the beginning, certainly, but not the end; it finds expression in the ordered disciplines of all the arts – the poet's words, the painter's colours, the musician's melodies, and harmonies. And St Thomas is surely right in saying that the essential quality of these arts must be *claritas*, lucidity. Inspiration is the beginning, but not the end: it must find expression in the disciplines of the ordered life, clear and definite.

Thus the Church, born in the ecstasy of Pentecost, finds interpretation and takes the disciplined and ordered forms of institution. You can think of it as a great procession, like 'an army, terrible with banners', says a medieval hymn writer – radiant and resplendent with all the Spirit's gifts, 'bringing many souls to glory.' Sometimes, perhaps, when we think of the contemporary Church, that vision tends to fade, and we have instead the impression of a drunken mob. We hear of liturgical anarchists who think they can and ought to write new prayer books every week; and stubborn reactionaries like myself, who think they can live in the Middle Ages, when God knew Latin best! Some school themselves in the latest dogmas of the sociologists, and others claim St Athanasius as the final theologian. The life of the Church seems full of confusion, and conflict, and opposition. 'Diversity of gifts' perhaps; but where is the unity of 'that one and self-same spirit that worketh all in all'? Are we bereft of the Spirit?

Confusion, controversies, and contradiction seem the

THE SOUL'S PILGRIMAGE

order of the day. But is that really a modern predicament? What is really new about it?

When we hail St Athanasius as champion of orthodoxy, do we forget that he was '*Athanasius contra mundum*' – 'Athanasius against the world' – exiled five times from Alexandria?

When our eyes drink in the glories of some magnificent medieval church, do we forget the cruel horrors of the Inquisition?

When we celebrate the fortitude of a Cranmer or a Ridley, can we say less of the fiery trials of a St John Fisher or St Thomas More? I could multiply examples endlessly from every period of our history. There are plenty of them, even within the New Testament: remember when St Paul 'withstood St Peter to his face'.

'Diversity of gifts' no doubt, but where is the unity of Spirit? And where is the promised truth, to which the Spirit leads? Where is the clarity, the order and lucidity?

I think the point is this: 'we know in part and prophesy in part.' Our treasure is in earthen vessels; our sight is dim and faith must celebrate our Lord in earthly forms of bread and wine. We do not grasp the whole of truth and sometimes not even that part at which we aim. The tower of finite understanding does not reach to heaven, and we fall back into a Babel of divided tongues. I do not mean that we have no Truth, or that our controversies are meaningless; 'we know in part.' I mean, rather, that it is only through the conflict and the opposition that the Spirit leads us on. I do not mean that our differences are unimportant; we must indeed 'test the spirits, whether they be of God', and follow the argument wherever it may lead. But we must also know the incompleteness of our grasp, and 'speak the truth in love'; and as St James advises us, be 'slow to speak and slow to wrath.' For, as a great medieval poet reminds us, 'I

PENTECOST / WHITSUNDAY

have seen the briar a prickly thing the winter through, and on its tip the very rose at close of spring.' After all, even our sins are within the economy of God's abounding grace, as wise St Paul informs us. And our present hope of heaven is not based on clear and perfect knowledge: 'Brethren, we know not what we shall be.'

What is required is that we be faithful to the Spirit's promptings, faithful to that truth we know, 'holding the mystery of faith in a pure conscience' and suffer the confusion of divided tongues. For only thus the Spirit leads us to all Truth; and one day 'we shall know as we are known'. We shall know with wholeness and completeness what now we know in part dividedly. Mockers within and without the Church will say our talk is incoherent, that we are confused like drunken men.

'But these are not drunken as ye suppose,' these are touched by Pentecost. Drunk, indeed, but not with wine; drunk, rather, with the Spirit of the Lord.

Amen.

TRINITY SUNDAY AND BAPTISM

*After this I saw, and behold,
a door was opened in heaven.*

With this great festival of the Holy Trinity which we celebrate today, the Church's year reaches a certain climax. Everything that has gone before leads up to this, points to this, and is fulfilled in this; for in this festival, we who are born anew of water and the Spirit, we who are risen with Christ, seeking the things which are above, we who are graced with God's Pentecostal Spirit, lift our gaze to look upon the mystery and majesty of God himself – God the Father, Son and Holy Spirit. This is not a festival which celebrates what God does; this is a festival which celebrates what God is. The spirit of this day is therefore the spirit of worship pure and simple, the spirit of adoration.

Most of our festivals are celebrations of the works of God – what God has done and does for us: his incarnation, his epiphany, his Passion and resurrection, his bestowal of his Holy Spirit. This one is different. This one invites us to lift our minds and hearts to contemplate, so far as human souls are capable, the very life of God Himself. That is the meaning of the scripture lessons appointed for today.

TRINITY SUNDAY AND BAPTISM

For the Epistle lesson, we have a portion of the vision of St John:

> After this I saw, and behold, a door was opened in heaven: and the first voice I heard was as it were of a trumpet talking with me; which said, 'Come up hither, and I will show thee things which must be hereafter.' And immediately I was in the Spirit; and behold, a throne was set in heaven, and one sat on the throne: and he that sat was to look upon like a jasper and a sardius stone: and a rainbow round about the throne, in sight like unto an emerald.

And so on. Well, it's a strange language, isn't it?

It's the poetic language of vision; it's the language of symbols, and poetic images, the language of imagination; the effort to speak in earthly terms of heavenly reality, which is infinitely beyond all earthly things. The language is obviously inadequate, as it must inevitably be. But it does catch some little hint of the glory and the majesty of God.

'Holy, Holy, Holy, Lord God the Almighty, which was, and which is, and which is to come.'

In the Gospel lesson, we have St John's account of Jesus' conversation with Nicodemus, the Pharisee, a leader of the Jews. The point Jesus makes is that true religion requires a new perspective, a new standpoint, a vision of heavenly things, a rebirth of the spirit. Nicodemus tries to draw the conversation back to familiar things, to bring it down to earth – he can't follow this 'highfaluting' talk. 'How can a man be born when he is old? Can he enter a second time into his mother's womb and be born?' But Jesus insists: unless a person be spiritually reborn, unless he or she can learn to look beyond earthly, fleshly, conventional, familiar things, they cannot see God's kingdom.

These scripture lessons, then, from Revelation and St John's Gospel, make essentially one point – one simple and all-important point: we who are reborn of water and the spirit (as these infants are today), we who are schooled in the truth of the Gospel of Jesus Christ must learn to fix our minds and hearts upon spiritual reality – the reality of God himself. That is our Christian training. That is our destiny in Christ. We must fix our minds and hearts in adoration of the glory and the majesty of God and live our lives in the light of that vision. That is the meaning of this festival.

When we speak of God as Holy Trinity, we speak the language of theology: we speak of God as Father – God as source and ground of being; we speak of God as Son – the eternally begotten Word, the perfection of all knowledge; we speak of God as Spirit – the eternal will of God, the perfection of all love. But whether or not we speak the language of theology in any sort of technical way, this doctrine and this festival have a very basic practical religious significance for each one of us.

To know God as absolute being, absolute knowledge, and absolute love, is to be spiritually reborn: it is to know ourselves as encompassed and upheld by providential care, and thus it is to see our own lives in a new spiritual perspective. It is to lose ourselves in the worship of a goodness and a glory infinitely beyond ourselves, infinitely beyond all earthly things, infinitely beyond all worldly pretensions and pettiness. It is to see our troubles, our frustrations, our disappointments, our ambitions and achievements, all in a new spiritual perspective – a radically different perspective – the perspective of eternity.

But perhaps we ask, with Nicodemus, 'Is this really possible? Is this really practical? Can a man be born when he is old? How

TRINITY SUNDAY AND BAPTISM

can these things be?' Nicodemus was a sensible man, no doubt: a Pharisee, a leader of the Jews, and he couldn't let go of his supposedly sensible, practical perspective. Jesus warned him, and Jesus warns us: unless you are spiritually reborn, you have no part in God's kingdom. 'That which is born of the flesh is flesh; and that which is born of the Spirit is spirit.'

Being born anew of the Spirit means a broadening and deepening of our minds, a refocusing of our loves: 'The wind bloweth where it listeth, and thou hearest the sound thereof, but canst not tell whence it cometh and whither it goeth; so is every one that is born of the Spirit.' The ways of spiritual life are very different from the ways of worldliness, and seem strange and unpredictable to worldly eyes. Nicodemus, in his worldly wisdom, does not understand. To him it seems visionary and impractical, and he will not venture.

This festival of God the Holy Trinity sets before our eyes an open door in heaven. 'Come up hither,' says the trumpet. We are called to fix our minds and hearts upon the majesty and mystery of God – to lose ourselves in adoration of a goodness and a glory immeasurably beyond all earthly imagining, and to live our lives in the light of that vision. 'So is every one that is born of the Spirit.'

'Behold a door was opened in heaven.'

Amen.

TRINITY SUNDAY

Behold, a door was opened in heaven.

For six months now, in the course of the Church's calendar, we have been remembering and celebrating the Incarnation and redeeming works of Christ our Saviour – all of it culminating in his glorious Ascension and the sending of the Holy Spirit. And the end of all this, the point of it all, is that we should come to know and love the living God, and thus fulfill our spiritual destiny, as sons. The Incarnation is the revelation of the life of God: his being, his eternal wisdom and his love. 'No man hath seen God at any time; but the only-begotten Son hath revealed him.' 'Behold, a door was opened in heaven.' The divine Spirit enables us to grasp that revelation, and to conform our lives to it, that we may attain the end of our redemption.

It is fitting, then, that our celebration of Christ's redeeming work should be summed up with the celebration of what is the whole point of it – the divine life of God himself, in which we are called to share: adoptive sons, by grace, 'heirs of God, and joint-heirs with Christ.'

The Scripture lessons for today have, therefore, a prophetic character: they speak to us of heavenly things. For the Epistle lesson, we have St John's thrilling vision of the heavenly throne. The angelic trumpet calls: 'Come up hither, and I will show thee things which must be hereafter.' And in the Gospel lesson, Jesus calls Nicodemus from earthly to heavenly things. You must have

TRINITY SUNDAY

a new standpoint, he tells him, 'You must be born again' and see with spiritual vision.

So today we who are born of the Spirit celebrate heavenly things. And that is no easy matter. The language of earth does not well suit the glories of heaven. We use the language of images and similes, and stretch imagination to the breaking point. St John is dazzled by his vision: 'He that sat upon the throne was to look upon like a jasper and a sardius stone … and a rainbow round about the throne like unto an emerald.' It is the language of imagination, the language of the earthly celebration of heavenly things, the language of poet and prophet.

But when we seek to explain the language of poetry and prophecy, we talk theology; and thus we speak of God the Holy Trinity. The doctrine of the Trinity is the central doctrine of the Christian faith. 'The Catholic faith is this,' says the Athanasian creed, 'that we worship one God in Trinity, and the Trinity in unity.' It is in that doctrine that Christian revelation brings all the speculations of religion to a certain clarity and completeness.

If you recall something of the early history of the Church, perhaps you know with what difficulty the doctrine of the Trinity was clarified. Perhaps you recall St. Athanasius, exiled five times from his diocese of Alexandria in his struggles against the Arians, who denied the doctrine. At one point it seemed to be *'Athanasius contra mundum'* – Athanasius against the world. All through the fourth century the Christian Empire was divided by an *'iota'* – the Greek letter 'i' – the difference between *'homoousios'* and *'homoiousios'*, the technical term whereby the orthodox said that the Son is of the same substance as the Father, very God, while the Arians said the Son is of like substance, not the same. That is why we say, in the Nicene Creed, 'being of one substance with the Father', 'very God of very God'. These are

THE SOUL'S PILGRIMAGE

phrases which pass glibly off our tongues, but they are phrases which were shouted by multitudes in processions through the streets of ancient Rome and Constantinople. The Arian solution – that Jesus is God-like, not very God, would have meant a very different Christianity. If he is not really God, he is not our saviour.

Perhaps to many modern Christians these seem mere technicalities, unnecessary details remote from the real business of Christianity – mere theological quibbles about a mystery which we can never penetrate. Yet how can we be satisfied with less than the truth revealed, and how can we be content to leave unconsidered the nature of the God we worship?

'We worship one God in Trinity, and the Trinity in unity,' says the Creed of St Athanasius. 'Three Persons and One God.' But what does that mean, beyond sheer mystification? There are certainly many homely images employed in an effort of explain. There is the venerable image of the shamrock – three leaves, and yet one leaf. There is the image of the man who has three characters – father to his children, husband to his wife, worker in his profession. Perhaps such illustrations help, but they certainly do not come very close to what we want to say; and often they are misleading, and even downright heretical – Arian, or worse!

St Augustine does better. He asks us to consider the life of the human soul, God's image. The soul remembers, it knows, it loves. These are three activities, and yet they are the activity of one soul. In us, these personal activities are an imperfect unity – our reason and our love do not simply coincide. God is the perfect unity of personal activity: He is, He knows, He loves; and with Him these three are one. Father, Word, and Spirit, three persons and one God: all equally divine, all absolutely God, one substance, one reality. God is not three beings, three

TRINITY SUNDAY

'personalities': God is one. Yet his unity is not a dead and static thing – He is the living God. His is the unity of personal activity: He is, He knows, He loves, eternally; and with God these personal activities, these 'persons' have a unity and equality towards which we can only strive. Our life is ever an imitation of that perfect life in which we are called to share as sons.

To us, God's life remains a mystery. But that does not mean that we understand nothing, that we 'ignorantly worship'. It means that we understand imperfectly a truth which exceeds our comprehension; and our knowing ends in the worship of a glory which remains always beyond it. And thus we return to the language of poetry and prophecy. 'Behold, a door is opened in heaven' and we catch a glimpse of the majesty of God.

> Cherubim and seraphim
> Veil their faces with the wings;
> Eyes of angels are too dim
> To behold the king of kings,
> While they sing eternally
> To the Blessed Trinity.

Amen.

NOTES

SUNDAY NEXT BEFORE ADVENT THE FEAST OF
CHRIST THE KING
Scripture: Jeremiah 23:5–8; John 1:35–45. Epigraph: John 6:12.
Preached 1999, All Saints, Oklahoma City, Oklahoma.

'He reigns and triumphs from the Tree,' Fortunatus, 'The royal banners forward go,' trans. Percy Dearmer, in *The Book of Common Praise: The Hymn Book of the Anglican Church of Canada* 1938, Toronto: Anglican Book Centre, No.128.

ADVENT I
Scripture: Romans 13:8–14; Matthew 21:1–13. Epigraph: Matthew 21:13. Preached 1999, St Alban's Cathedral, Prince Albert, Saskatchewan.

ADVENT I SECOND SERMON
Scripture: Romans 13:8–14; Matthew 21:1–13. Epigraph: Romans 13:8. Preached 1974, Holy Trinity, Bridgewater, Nova Scotia.

ADVENT II
Scripture: Romans 15:4–13; Luke 21:25–33. Epigraph: Luke 21:28. Preached 2000, St George's, Halifax, Nova Scotia.

'And lo, already on the hills…,' 'Thy Kingdom Come! On Bended Knee,' Frederick L. Hesmer (1840-1929), 1881. (https://hymnary.org/text/thy_kingdom_come_on_bended_knee)

THE SOUL'S PILGRIMAGE

'O see, so many worlds of barren years...,' *Carmen Deo Nostro*, 'To the Name, Above Every Name, the Name of Jesus,' Richard Crashaw (1613-1649), *The Complete Works of Richard Crashaw, Volume I*, 2012, London: Robson and Sons, Alexander Balloch Grosart, ed. https://www.gutenberg.org/files/38549/38549-h/38549-h.htm. (140-148).

ADVENT III
Scripture: 1 Corinthians 4:1–5; Matthew 11:2–10. Epigraph: 1 Corinthians 4:2. Preached 1978, St James', Halifax, Nova Scotia.

'Happy those servants ...,' *'Nocte Surgentes,'* trans. Robert Bridges, in *The Book of Common Praise: The Hymn Book of the Anglican Church of Canada* 1938, Toronto: Anglican Book Centre, No. 813.

ADVENT IV
Scripture: Philippians 4:4–7; John 1:19–29. Epigraph: John 1:33. Preached 1982, St James', Halifax, Nova Scotia.

'The whole life of Christ...' John Donne, 'Preached at S. Paul's upon Christmas Day, 1626,' in *The Sermons of John Donne, vol.VII*, 1962, ed. Evelyn M. Simpson and George R. Potter. Berkeley: University of California Press, no. 11, p. 279.

'The holly bears a berry...' Trad. 'The Holly and the Ivy', in *English Folk Carols,* 1911, ed. Cecil Sharp. London: Novello & Co, Ltd., no. VII.

NOTES

CHRISTMAS
Scripture: Hebrews 1:1-12; John 1:1-14. Epigraph: John 1:14. Preached 1955, St Clement's, Toronto, Ontario.

THE OCTAVE DAY OF CHRISTMAS / THE CIRCUMCISION OF CHRIST
Scripture: Isaiah 9:2–7; Luke 2:15–21. Epigraph: Isaiah 9:2. Preached 1982, St James', Halifax, Nova Scotia.

Bede, *Ecclesiastical History of the English Nation*, 1962, trans. J. E. King. Cambridge, Massachusetts: Harvard University Press, p. 281–283.

EPIPHANY
Scripture: Ephesians 3:1–12; Matthew 2:1–12. Epigraph: Matthew 2:12. Preached 2004, St John's, Savannah, Georgia.

'A cold coming we had of it …', T. S. Eliot, 'Journey of the Magi' in *Selected Poems* 1954, London: Faber & Faber.

'Sermon for Christmas Day 1622', from Lancelot Andrewes, 'Sermon XV', *Sermons on the Nativity*, 1955, Grand Rapids: Baker Book House.

> Last we consider the time of their coming, the season of the year. It was no summer progress. A cold coming they had of it at this time of the year, just the worst time of the year to take a journey, and specially a long journey in. The ways deep, the weather sharp, the days short, the sun farthest off, *in solstitio brumali*, 'the very dead of winter.' *Venimus*, 'we are come,' if that be

THE SOUL'S PILGRIMAGE

one, *venimus*, 'we are now come,' come at this time, that sure is another.

T. S. Eliot, 'The Waste Land' in *Selected Poems*, London: Faber and Faber Ltd, 1954, pp. 97-98. Used by permission.

THE BAPTISM OF OUR LORD FIRST SERMON
Scripture: Isaiah 42:1-8; Mark 1:1-11. Epigraph: John 3:5. Preached 1979, St James', Halifax, Nova Scotia.

'Brightest and best of the sons of the morning,' Reginald Heber 1811 in *The Book of Common Praise: The Hymn Book of the Anglican Church of Canada*, 1938, Toronto: Anglican Book Centre, No. 356.

'... not by the conversion of the Godhead into the flesh'... Creed of St Athanasius, *Book of Common Prayer, 1959*, Toronto, Anglican Church of Canada, p.697.

THE BAPTISM OF OUR LORD SECOND SERMON
Scripture: Isaiah 42:1-8; Mark 1:1-11. Epigraph: John 3:6. Preached 1983, King's College Chapel, Halifax, Nova Scotia.

EPIPHANY I
Scripture: Romans 12:1–5; Luke 2:41–52. Epigraph: Romans 12:2. Preached 1998, St Aidan's, Toronto, Ontario.

EPIPHANY II
Scripture: Romans 12:6–16; John 2:1–11. Epigraph: John 2:11. Preached 1978, St James', Halifax, Nova Scotia.

NOTES

Crouse may be using his own translation and excerpts from St Thomas Aquinas, *Commentary* on 2 Cor 5.16-17:

> Creatio enim est motus ex nihilo ad esse. Est autem duplex esse, scilicet esse naturae et esse gratiae. Prima creatio facta fuit quando creaturae ex nihilo productae sunt a Deo in esse naturae, et tunc creatura erat nova, sed tamen per peccatum inveterata est. Thren. III, 4: *vetustam fecit pellem meam*, et cetera. Oportuit ergo esse novam creationem, per quam producerentur in esse gratiae, quae quidem creatio est ex nihilo, quia qui gratia carent, nihil sunt. I Cor. XIII, v. 2: *si noverim mysteria omnia*, etc., *charitatem autem non habeam*, et cetera. Iob XVIII, v. 15: *habitent in tabernaculo illius socii eius, qui non est*, id est peccati. Augustinus dicit: *peccatum enim nihil est, et nihili fiunt homines cum peccant*. Et sic patet, quod infusio gratiae est quaedam creatio (St Thomas Aquinas, *Commentary* on 2 Corinthians 5.16-17).

EPIPHANY III
Scripture: Romans 12:16–21; Matthew 8:1–13. Epigraph: Romans 12:16. Preached 1998, King's College Chapel, Halifax, Nova Scotia.

CANDLEMAS / PURIFICATION OF THE BLESSED VIRGIN MARY / THE PRESENTATION OF CHRIST IN THE TEMPLE
Scripture: Malachi 3:1–5; Luke 2:22–40. Epigraph: Ephesians 5:8. Preached 1985, St James', Halifax, Nova Scotia.

'our bread is blessed by light....' Crouse reminds us of the marvellous poem 'Bread and Wine' written in 1801 by Frederick

THE SOUL'S PILGRIMAGE

Holderlin (1770-1843) to encourage us to wait in hope, like the aged Simeon, for the one who will come and redeem Israel, and each one of us.

> The choir of gods left some gifts behind, as a sign
> Of their presence and eventual return, which we
> May appreciate in our human fashion, as we used to.
> That which is superior had grown too great for pleasure
> With spirit among men. And to this day no one's
> strong enough. For the highest joys, although
> some gratitude survives quietly. Bread is the
> fruit of the earth, yet it's blessed also by light.
> The pleasure of wine comes from the thundering god.
> We remember the gods thereby, those who were once
> With us, and who'll return when the time is right.
> Thus poets sing of the wine god in earnest, and their
> Ringing praises of the old one aren't devised in vain.

Poems of Friedrich Hölderlin, 2022 San Francisco, Ithuriel's Spear, trans. James Mitchell, section 8, lines 7 - 18, p. 21.

CANDLEMAS SECOND SERMON
Scripture: Malachi 3:1-5; Luke 2:22-40. Epigraph: Luke 2:30. Preached 1976, St James, Halifax, Nova Scotia.

EPIPHANY V
Scripture: Colossians 3:12–17; Matthew 13:24–30. Epigraph: Colossians 3:14. Preached 1992, King's College Chapel, Halifax, Nova Scotia.

NOTES

'Let no one be too self-assured…,' Dante Alighieri, *Paradiso*, 1943, trans. Laurence Binyon. London: Macmillan & Co., XIII.130-135.

In these lines of Dante's *Paradiso*, Thomas Aquinas continues to guide the poetical character, Dante, by warning him against unreasoned and hasty judgements.

SEPTUAGESIMA FIRST SERMON
Scripture: 1 Corinthians 9:24-27; Matthew 20:1-16. Epigraph: 1 Corinthians 9:24. Preached 1991, All Saints', Rome, Italy.

The Gulf War that Crouse refers to here began with Iraq's invasion of Kuwait in 1990 and escalated into an international conflict.

SEPTUAGESIMA SECOND SERMON
Scripture: 1 Corinthians 9:24-27; Matthew 20:1-16. Epigraph: Matthew 20:6. Preached 1981, location unknown.

'Many keep company with God in word, but shun him in deed ….', St Gregory the Great, 'St Gregory: On The Gospel: Given to the People in the Basilica of the Blessed Laurence on Septuagesima Sunday,' *The Sunday Sermons of the Great Fathers*, vol. 1, 1957, trans. M.F. Toal, Chicago: Henry Regnery Co., pp. 382-383.

SEPTUAGESIMA THIRD SERMON
Scripture: 1 Corinthians 9:24-27; Matthew 20:1-16. Epigraph: Matthew 20:6. Preached 1982, St James', Halifax, Nova Scotia.

THE SOUL'S PILGRIMAGE

'Those trifles of all trifles'... Augustine, *Confessions* VIII xi

...the world is too much with us , William Wordsworth, *Poems in Two Volumes,* vol. 2, 1807, London: Longman, Hurst, Rees, and Orme.

SEXAGESIMA
Scripture: 2 Corinthians 11:21–31; Luke 8:4–15. Epigraph: Luke 8:15. Preached 1983, St James', Halifax, Nova Scotia.

QUINQUAGESIMA
Scripture: 1 Corinthians 13:1–13; Luke 18:31–43. Epigraph: Luke 18:31. Preached in an unknown location, date unknown.

The collect for Quinquagesima:
> O Lord, who has taught us that all our doings without charity are nothing worth: Send thy Holy Spirit, and pour into our hearts that most excellent gift of charity, the very bond of peace and of all virtues, without which whosoever liveth is counted dead before thee. Grant this for thine only Son Jesus' Christ's sake. Amen.

ASH WEDNESDAY
Scripture: James 4:6–11; Matthew 6:16–21. Epigraph: Matthew 6:21. Preached 1999, King's College Chapel, Halifax, Nova Scotia.

LENT I
Scripture: 2 Corinthians 6:1–10; Matthew 4:1–11. Epigraph: Matthew 4:1. Preached 1979, St James', Halifax, Nova Scotia.

NOTES

See Gen. 3:5. 'For God doth know that in the day ye eat thereof, then your eyes shall be opened, and ye shall be as gods, knowing good and evil.'

LENT II
Scripture: 1 Thessalonians 4:1–7; Matthew 15:21–28. Epigraph: Matthew 15:28. Preached 1989, St George's, Halifax, Nova Scotia.

LENT III
Scripture: Ephesians 5:1–14; Luke 11:14–26. Epigraph: Luke 11:21. Preached 1979, St James', Halifax, Nova Scotia.

See Isa. 14:12-14. 'How art thou fallen from heaven, O Lucifer, son of the morning! how art thou cut down to the ground, which didst weaken the nations! For thou hast said in thine heart, I will ascend into heaven, I will exalt my throne above the stars of God: I will sit also upon the mount of the congregation, in the sides of the north: I will ascend above the heights of the clouds; I will be like the most High.'

'And were this world all devils o'er...', Martin Luther, 'A safe stronghold our God is still,' trans. Thomas Carlyle, in *The Book of Common Praise: The Hymn Book of the Anglican Church of Canada 1938*, Toronto: Anglican Book Centre, No. 405.

President Eisenhower used this quote numerous times in speeches that are recorded in his electronic archive: https://www.eisenhowerlibrary.gov/search/When%20a%20strong%20man%20armed%20keepeth%20his%20house

THE SOUL'S PILGRIMAGE

LENT IV
Scripture: Galatians 4:26–5:1; John 6:5–14. Epigraph: Galatians 5:1. Preached 1978, St James', Halifax, Nova Scotia.

The Collect for Fourth Sunday in Lent:
'Grant, we beseech thee, Almighty God, that we, who for our evil deeds do worthily deserve to be punished, by the comfort of thy grace may mercifully be relieved; through our Lord and Saviour Jesus Christ. Amen.' *The Book of Common Prayer* 1962, Toronto: Anglican Book Centre, p. 147. See Rom. 8:16–17

'Brief life is here our portion…,' Bernard of Cluny, 'Brief life is here our portion', trans. J.M. Neale, in *The Book of Common Praise: The Hymn Book of the Anglican Church of Canada* 1938, Toronto: Anglican Book Centre, No. 626.

PASSION SUNDAY FIRST SERMON
Hebrews 9:11–15; Matthew 20:20–28. Epigraph: Matthew 20:26. Preached 1981, St James', Halifax, Nova Scotia.

'Fulfilled is all his words foretold.' Fortunatus, 'The royal banners forward go', trans. Percy Dearmer, in *The Book of Common Praise: The Hymn Book of the Anglican Church of Canada* 1938, Toronto: Anglican Book Centre, No. 128.

PASSION SUNDAY SECOND SERMON
Scripture: Epigraph: Matthew 20:25
Preached 2006, King's College Chapel, Halifax, Nova Scotia.

PALM SUNDAY
Scripture: Philippians 2:5–11; Matthew 27:1–54. Epigraph:

NOTES

Philippians 2:5. Preached 2002, Christ Church Cathedral, Victoria, British Columbia.

The 'triumphal entry' Gospel is Matthew 21:1-11 which is read as a separate Gospel in addition to the Passion Gospel read in the Holy Communion itself. This short 'Gospel of the Palms' is read before the procession begins.

'Sometimes they strew his way.' Dean Samuel Crossman, 'My song is love unknown', in *The Book of Common Praise: The Hymn Book of the Anglican Church of Canada* 1938, Toronto: Anglican Book Centre, No. 596.

'Fulfilled is all his words foretold.' Fortunatus, 'The Royal Banners Forward Go', trans. Percy Dearmer, in *The Book of Common Praise: The Hymn Book of the Anglican Church of Canada* 1938, Toronto: Anglican Book Centre, No. 128.

TUESDAY IN HOLY WEEK
Scripture: Isaiah 49: 1-7; 1 Corinthians 1:18-42; John 12:20-36. Epigraph: Isaiah 50. Preached 1982, location unknown.

'Why, what hath my Lord done?' Dean Samuel Crossman, 'My song is love unknown', in *The Book of Common Praise: The Hymn Book of the Anglican Church of Canada* 1938, Toronto: Anglican Book Centre, No. 596.

'O Tree of Grace, the conquering sign,' Fortunatus, from 'The Royal Banners Forward Go,' trans. Percy Dearmer, in *The Book of Common Praise: The Hymn Book of the Anglican Church of Canada* 1938, Toronto: Anglican Book Centre, No. 128.

THE SOUL'S PILGRIMAGE

MAUNDY THURSDAY FIRST SERMON
Scripture: 1 Corinthians 11:23–29; Luke 23:1–49. Epigraph: John 15:15. Preached 1980, King's College Chapel, Halifax, Nova Scotia.

'That was all the work of Gods,' Homer, *The Odyssey*, 1998, trans. Robert Fitzgerald, New York: Farrar, Strauss, and Giroux, VIII.619–620.

'When there is a great interval...,' Aristotle, *Nicomachean Ethics*, 1984, in *The Complete Works of Aristotle*, the revised Oxford translation, Princeton University Press. VIII.7.

'... and leave the altar bare and cold.' Here Crouse refers to the movement within the Maundy Thursday liturgy at which he is preaching: later on in the service, the hangings that adorn the altar will be removed, leaving the bare wood of the altar exposed.

MAUNDY THURSDAY SECOND SERMON
Scripture: 1 Corinthians 11:23–29; Luke 23:1–49. Epigraph: II Corinthians 5:14. Preached 1984, King's College Chapel, Halifax, Nova Scotia.

GOOD FRIDAY
Scripture: Hebrews 10:1-25; John 18:33-19:37. Epigraph: Luke 18:31-34. Preached 1982, St James', Halifax, Nova Scotia.

'Who was the guilty, who brought this upon thee?'. Johann Heermann, 'Ah, holy Jesu, how hast thou offended,' trans. Robert Bridges, in *The Book of Common Praise: The Hymn Book*

NOTES

of the Anglican Church of Canada 1938, Toronto: Anglican Book Centre, No. 108.

'Alas, sweet lord, what were't to thee.' Richard Crashaw, '*Charitas Nimia*, or The Dear Bargain,' in *The Oxford Book of Christian Verse,* 1973, ed. Lord David Cecil. Oxford: Clarendon Press, no. 143, p. 206-207.

'My Song is Love Unknown.' Dean Samuel Crossman, 'My song is love unknown,' in *The Book of Common Praise: The Hymn Book of the Anglican Church of Canada* 1938, Toronto: Anglican Book Centre, No. 596.

EASTER DAY
Scripture: Colossians 3:1–11; John 20:1–10. Epigraph: James 1:18. Preached date unknown, St Peter's Cathedral, Charlottetown, Prince Edward Island.

'Welcome, happy morning!'. Fortunatus, 'Welcome, happy morning!,' trans. John Ellerton, in *The Book of Common Praise: The Hymn Book of the Anglican Church of Canada* 1938, Toronto: Anglican Book Centre, No. 168.

'…this favoured island and this gloriously decorated church': Crouse refers here to Prince Edward Island and to St Peter's Cathedral in Charlottetown.

'…all this juice and all this joy,'. Gerard Manley Hopkins, 'Spring,' in *The Oxford Book of Christian Verse,* 1973, ed. Lord David Cecil, Oxford: Clarendon Press, no. 320, p. 496.

THE SOUL'S PILGRIMAGE

'April is the cruellest month.' T.S. Eliot, 'The Waste Land,' in *Selected Poems* 1954, London: Faber & Faber, 'The Burial of the Dead,' lines 1–2.

'I have seen the briar ....'. Dante, *Paradise,* trans. Sayers and Reynolds, 1962, London, Penguin Books, XIII.133–135.

EASTER MONDAY
Scripture: Acts 10:34–43; Luke 24:13–35. Epigraph: Luke 24:21. Preached 1996, St Thomas's, Toronto, Ontario.

See the final chorus of Bach's St John Passion, *Ruht wohl* ('Rest well'), sung after Jesus' burial. In comparing the opening chorus of the Cantata *Bleib bei uns* to the *Ruht wohl* of the St. John Passion, Crouse is saying that Bach used his compositions to draw a theological link between the disciples' grief at Jesus' tomb and their 'bewilderment' in the story of the Road to Emmaus.

'But, O my father, is it thinkable…"'. Virgil, *The Aeneid,* 1951 trans. Rolfe Humphries, New York: Charles Scribner's Sons, Book VI, p. 168.

'Time, like an ever-rolling stream', Isaac Watts, 'O God, our help in ages past', in *The Book of Common Praise: The Hymn Book of the Anglican Church of Canada* 1938, Toronto: Anglican Book Centre, No. 379.

'…reclothed in the holy and glorious flesh', Dante, *Paradise,* 1962, trans. Sayers and Reynolds, 1962, London: Penguin Books, XIV. 43–44.

NOTES

EASTER I
Scripture: 1 John 5.4-12; John 20.19-23. Epigraph: Zechariah 12:10. Preached 1982, St James', Halifax, Nova Scotia.

'O all-sufficient sacrifice', 'The Lamb's high banquet called to share', trans J.M. Neale, in *The Book of Common Praise: The Hymn Book of the Anglican Church of Canada* 1938, Toronto: Anglican Book Centre, No. 158.

'Let holy charity', Bianco da Siena, 'Come down, O Love divine', trans. Richard Frederick Littledale, in *The Book of Common Praise: The Hymn Book of the Anglican Church of Canada* 1938, Toronto: Anglican Book Centre, No. 175a.

EASTER II
Scripture: 1 Peter 2:19–25; John 10:11–16. Epigraph: Psalm 23:1. Preached 1981, St James', Halifax, Nova Scotia.

'You imagine that a shepherd studies the interests of his flocks,' Plato, *Republic*, trans. Cornford, 1941, London, Oxford University Press, 343b.

EASTER III
Scripture: 1 Peter 2:11–17; John 16:16–22. Epigraph: John 16:16. Preached in unknown location, date unknown.

EASTER IV FIRST SERMON
Scripture: James 1:17–21; John 16:5–14. Epigraph: John 16:7. Preached 1981, St James', Halifax, Nova Scotia.

THE SOUL'S PILGRIMAGE

EASTER IV SECOND SERMON
Scripture: James 1:17–21; John 16:5–14. Epigraph: John 16:7. in unknown location, date unknown.

'Grant, Father, to my mind', Boethius, *Consolation of Philosophy*, III, m.9, trans. Robert Crouse.

EASTER V/ROGATION
Scripture Lessons: James 1:22–27; John 16:23–33. Epigraph: Romans 8:22. Preached in unknown location, date unknown.

Gerard Manley Hopkins, 'God's Grandeur':

> The world is charged with the grandeur of God.
>   It will flame out, like shining from shook foil;
>   It gathers to a greatness, like the ooze of oil
> Crushed. Why do men then now not reck his rod?
> Generations have trod, have trod, have trod;
>   And all is seared with trade; bleared, smeared with toil;
>   And wears man's smudge and shares man's smell: the soil
> Is bare now, nor can foot feel, being shod.

Gerard Manley Hopkins*: Poems and Prose* 1985, London: Penguin Classics.

Paul Claudel, *Conversations dans le Loir-et-Cher* from a passage that continues:

> Everything that the creative Word has brought forth must in the end hear also the redemptive Word, that nothing in his creation be stranger to his revelation in glory. Before

NOTES

that solemn mass begin, all the aisles of creation must be cleared that the Priest may pass freely from one end of the church to the other in order to baptize all, while the children of God intone the *Vidi aquam* and the Asperges [from the cosmic liturgy of the resurrection].

In George H. Williams, *Wilderness and Paradise in Christian Thought,* 2016, Eugene, Wipf and Stock.

ASCENSION
Scripture: Acts 1:1–11; Mark 16:14–20. Epigraph: Acts 1:11. Preached 1984, St James', Halifax, Nova Scotia.

'All creatures of our God and King,' Paraphraser William H. Draper; Author St. Francis of Assisi, 1225, in *The Book of Common Praise: The Hymn Book of the Anglican Church of Canada* 1938, Toronto: Anglican Book Centre, No. 355.

'O choose ye then...' Edward Bouverie Pusey, 'Sermon XXI: Heaven the Christian's Home', *Sermons During the Season from Advent to Whitsuntide,* 1848, Oxford: J.H. Parker, p. 340.

SUNDAY AFTER THE ASCENSION
Scripture: 1 Peter 4.7-1; John 15.26-16:4. Epigraph: John 3:6. Preached 1980, St James', Halifax, Nova Scotia.

'Yea, angels tremble when they see', 'Eternal Monarch, King Most High', trans J.M. Neale, in *The Book of Common Praise: The Hymn Book of the Anglican Church of Canada* 1938, Toronto: Anglican Book Centre, No. 835.

THE SOUL'S PILGRIMAGE

'See the Conqueror mounts in triumph He has raised our human nature', see the king in royal state,' Christopher Wordsworth (1862), in *The Book of Common Praise: The Hymn Book of the Anglican Church of Canada* 1938, Toronto: Anglican Book Centre, No. d498.

PENTECOST / WHITSUNDAY
Scripture Lessons: Acts 2:1–11; John 14:15-27. Epigraph: John 3:6.

Scripture: Revelation 4:1–11; John 3:1–16. Epigraph: John 4:24; John 4:23; John 14. Preached 'in sudden torrents dread', John Keble, 'Whitsunday'.

TRINITY SUNDAY AND BAPTISM
Scripture: Revelation 4:1–11; John 3:1–16. Epigraph: Revelation 4:1. Preached 1985, St James', La Have, Nova Scotia.

TRINITY SUNDAY
Scripture: Revelation 4:1-11. Epigraph: Revelation 4:1. Preached 1980, St James', La Have, Nova Scotia.

LIST OF ILLUSTRATIONS

FRONTISPIECE
Anon, *Tree of Life* mosaic, 1120-1128 (San Clemente, Rome). Photograph: Jastrow, 2006, public domain: https://commons.wikimedia.org/wiki/File:Apsis_mosaic_San_Clemente.jpg

Timeline
Timeline graphic design: Morgan Rogers, co & co, Halifax, N.S.

NASA and the Space Telescope Science Institute, *Star Dying*, Webb Space Telescope photograph, March 14, 2023, (Sun's orbit), https://webbtelescope.org/contents/media/images/2023/111/01GTWASGERK0M8G86WZZSRC1ZX?fbclid=IwAR0wQW-Hge-FsRjWMTttki3IIfydYX6iKpVx2HwWeSznOkHWiWdDhD97c10&news=true

The Nativity, Icon, c1475, (Gostinopolye Church of St. Nicholas) Public Domain, Attribution: https://commons.wikimedia.org/wiki/File:Nativity_from_Gostinopolye_(c._1475,_Banco_Intesa).jpg

Jesus Teaching in the Temple, stained glass window, (University of King's College chapel, Halifax, Canada). Attribution: photo by Lokwing Wong

THE SOUL'S PILGRIMAGE

Van Gogh, Vincent, *The Sower*, oil on canvas, 1888 (Kroller Muller Gallery, Otterlo, Netherlands) 64,2x80,3 cm https://commons.wikimedia.org/wiki/File:Vincent_van_Gogh_-_The_Sower_-_c._17-28_June_1888.jpg

Munch, Edvard, *The Scream,* oil, tempera, pastels and crayon on cardboard, 1893 91cmx73.5 cm, (National Gallery, Oslo, Norway) https://en.wikipedia.org/wiki/The_Scream#/media/File:Edvard_Munch,_1893,_The_Scream,_oil,_tempera_and_pastel_on_cardboard,_91_x_73_cm,_National_Gallery_of_Norway.jpg

Master of the Lehman Crucifixion, *Noli me Tangere,* fresco, active c. 1352-1399, (National Gallery) 542x800. Wikidata: https://www.wikidata.org/wiki/Q26692367

Anonymous. *The Good Shepherd,* mosaic, c. 400 (Mausoleum of Galla Placidia), photograph from Wikipedia, by Petar Milošević

St Francis Master/Giotto, *Legend of St Francis #15 Sermon to the Birds,* 1297-1300 (Basilica de San Francesco, Assisi). https://commons.wikimedia.org/wiki/Saint_Francis_cycle_in_the_Upper_Church_of_San_Francesco_at_Assisi#:~:text=The%20legend%20of%20Saint%20Francis,the%20walls%20of%20the%20transept.

Doré, Gustave, *Par, 31 Rosa celeste*, ink drawing in Alighieri, Dante. 1892. *The Divine Comedy*, trans. Henry Francis Cary ed., London, Paris & Melbourne: Cassell & Company (Retrieved on 13 July 2009).

LIST OF ILLUSTRATIONS

Labyrinth pavement, early 13th century, Chartres Cathedral. Photo: EinDao, 20 January, 2019. https://commons.wikimedia.org/wiki/File:Labyrinth_der_Kathedrale_von_Notre-Dame_de_Chartres_in_Stein.jpg

IMAGES IN TEXT VOL. I
Giovanni Pisano, 'Adoration of the Magi', 1298-1301, pulpit and relief, Sant'Andrea, Pistoia. Photo by Saiko, 2018, used by permission under the Creative Commons license.

Raphael, The School of Athens, 1509-1511, fresco, (Apostolic Palace, Vatican City).https://commons.wikimedia.org/w/index.php?curid=4406048